Out of the Mouth of Babes...

A Little Book of Sunshine

Marika Lee Connole
Phoenix, Arizona

Published by Lulu
October of 2009.

ISBN 978-1-4357-3074-8

Table of Contents

~ Chapter 1

Where It All Began

It all started in the summer of 1992. I had my hands full—literally. My hands were full of babies. I had a two year old, a one year old and a two month old.

Somehow in between changing diapers, feeding, clothing, changing diapers, bathing, cleaning, changing diapers, and more diapers, I realized that my babies would grow up quickly. I decided that one of the best things that I could do would be to write down cute things they said and did. I also wanted to include milestones and other information.

As it turned out, the one thing that could always make me pull out the kid's journal was the cute things that would spew forth from their mouths. Thus, it went from a kid's journal to a funny-things-the-kids-say journal. I regret the fact that I know I missed several funny things. I am happy to know that I recorded as many as I did because my children love to peruse the pages of the journal, keeping an eye open especially for things pertaining to themselves!

One day, as I was looking back over all the journal entries myself, I realized that I had plenty of material for a book. It would be a book reminiscent of Art Linkletter's "Kids Say the Darndest Things".

I am fortunate enough to own a copy of said book. It was printed in 1957 with drawings by Charles M. Shulz of "Peanuts" fame. Because I love the descriptive way children are presented in the introduction, I must quote a little of it.

> Here is the exciting play of fanciful imagination, of lively curiosity, of the need to find out, to seem wise beyond their years. Here is the nonsense that sometimes makes strange sense, the quick inventions, the unconscious witticisms—the wonderful, intimate revelation of childhood in honest, funny, sometimes pathetic sayings about itself.
>
> It is a shame that we must lose this forthright honesty, this searching curiosity, this drive of the imagination toward great deeds, exciting adventure, knowledge, achievements to win fame and honors and pleasure, in the process of "growing up."
>
> These are the qualities which the inventors retain, men like Edison, Fulton, DeForest—artists, poets, musicians, scientists, naturalists. The natural heritage of children.
>
> Age has nothing to do with it; I mean the actual years. It is the conventions, the expected staid behavior of adults, the embarrassment at being thought "childish," which finally cramps down our imaginative flights and inventive curiosity.
>
> I myself have been flattered by the reputation for never having quite grown up…

Who is the author of the introduction? None other than the ultimate kid himself, Walt Disney! Doesn't he describe children well?

I have seen so much of these things in my own children. Children are amazing creatures. It is no wonder that the Bible admonishes us in Matthew 18:3, "Verily I say unto you, Except ye be converted, and become as little children, ye shall not enter into the kingdom of heaven."

The scriptures also tell us in Isaiah 11:6 that, "The wolf also shall dwell with the lamb, and the leopard shall lie down with the kid; and the calf and the young lion and the fatling together; and a little child shall lead them." Boy, do I believe that to be true. I have learned so much from my little crew as they lead by their example.

On the pages that follow, I will share with you some truths that have been taught to me or reinforced by my children. There's never a dull moment around here. Over the course of the 16 years since I began journaling my children's humorous moments, I have collected enough anecdotes to fill pages and pages. There are 100's of entries. I do hope you have even half as much fun reading them as I have had.

Let me clarify a few things to make the reading a little easier. First of all, we have 7 children that currently range in age from 19 to 17 months. When relating a tale about one of the children, I put a number (4) in parentheses to indicate the age of the child at that time. I could have left all the dates in there and let you do the math yourself, but, this book is supposed to be fun, not work! ;)

Second, we belong to The Church of Jesus Christ of Latter-Day Saints, commonly called—"The Mormon Church". Some of the funnies have to do with things our kids have said that pertain to this church. I do my best to explain gospel principles if necessary. (You can go to these official

Church websites www.mormon.org or www.lds.org for more information.)

Third, to protect the privacy of extended family members, friends and acquaintances that may have found their way in to this book, I will not refer to those people by name.

Fourth, my children are of Swedish ancestry and therefore refer to my parents as Morfar (Grandpa) and Mormor (Grandma). My husband's parents have the usual Grandpa/Grandma designation.

Fifth, I am not worrying about being politically correct or anything like that, so please—take all this with a grain of salt. Children are innocent & naïve and will say and do things that grown-ups would never dream of!

Whew! I think that is it. Are you ready for a little fun?

~ Chapter 2

Have a Little Fun & Enjoy Life

Children have a way of coming up with some of the funniest things without even trying. Sometimes I take life a little too seriously. My kids help me to lighten up by doing things like this:

> Out of the blue, Manda (3 ½) came to Daddy and said, "You have to laugh Dad."
>
> So Dad did.
>
> Then Manda says, "What's so funny, Dad?"

Or by being imaginative.

> Amanda (3) insists that she has a "rainbow head" as opposed to a forehead.

I have to remember to just have a little fun like Amanda.

> The kids were playing "guess what animal I am" with two of their Aunts. One Aunt had been whispering some things to Brayden (2 ½) that he could pretend to be, keeping it a secret from the other aunt. On her next turn, Amanda (3

½) went running to Aunty #1 and says, "Tell me a pig!"

I learned from Patrik that you can find humor in strange places.

We were looking at Daddy's bottom teeth. He has one tooth that is situated behind the others. Patrik (5) came over to see. He started giggling and said, "Oh look! That one is getting away!"

Who shouldn't enjoy a good, genuine prank on occasion?

Brayden (3) came and told me he had "peed in his pants". I was surprised because he usually doesn't have accidents and on the rare occasion that he does, he gets terribly upset with himself. This time he was almost smiling. I didn't believe he had done it, so I questioned him again and he said, "Mmmhmmn, just a widdle bit".

So I checked and sure enough his pants were wet. So I started taking them off while he was still in very good spirits. I told him it isn't something to be so happy about. After I got the pants off, I checked the underwear, which were completely dry! I said, "Brayden! You didn't pee your pants!"

He says, "No, I poured water down my leg." What a tease! That he could even think of such a trick at 3 years old!

And that was just the beginning with him. The 3-year-old prankster kept at it through the years...

This morning I heard a loud gasp from the bathroom shortly after Kevin went to take a shower. When I inquired about it afterwards, Kevin told me this, "I cleaned out all the toys from the tub, turned on the water, and pulled the shower curtain closed. Then I went to get in--knowing I had gotten all the toys out--and THIS (he pulls out an ugly plastic spider) was in the tub!"

I later related this story to the kids at lunchtime because I got a kick out of it. I told the kids it was kind of funny because the spider was kind of stuck in the folds of the shower curtain and must have just fallen out when Dad pulled on the curtain.

Brayden (8) pipes up at this point and says with a grin, "Yeah, I put it there."

Not having thought previously that Dad was the victim of a prank, I was surprised and asked, "You did that on purpose?"

Brayden responded, "No."

I said, "You didn't mean to put it into the shower curtain?"

Brayden gleefully chortled, "Yes, I did, but it wasn't on purpose to get Dad. I was planning to get you, Mom!"

Then there are all the jokes kids love to tell. Here's one.

Here is a joke Malena (3 ½) told me.

"Q: When would a movie throw a bookcase at you?

A: RUN!!"

I suppose running is a good idea if a bookcase has been thrown at you!

Of course it is a good idea to be excited about silly games for a laugh.

Sean (9 months) likes to play a game where you put something on either his or your own head and then watch it fall off. He laughs like crazy at this.

One day as I was laying on the floor intent on my reading, Sean came to me. I tried to ignore him (impossibly). Next thing I know I have a paper plate on my head, which Sean is holding in place. I finally looked up at him and he had the cheesiest of grins on his face. He was ready to play. How could I resist?

You never know what is going to be good for a little snicker!

I was folding the laundry and the piles of folded clothing were around the Christmas tree. Sean (20 months) came in the room, looked at me with a silly smirk on his little face, and teasingly said, "Nice presents, Mom."

If something tickles your funny bone, share it! Everyone needs laughter.

Patrik (8 ½) was reading some information about cheetahs to the other kids. He found it amusing that they feed somewhat on game birds. In a jesting manner he said, "Oh, hey little game bird, do you want to play monopoly?"

Using your "poker face" can get you more mileage when telling jokes.

Brayden (6 ½) asked me if there were any such thing as real fairies. I said, "Not really."

Brayden thought a moment then exclaimed, "Oh yeah, there's the tooth fairy!"

And then he added with a completely straight face (no hint of a joke) "...and the chin fairy and the cheek fairy, and the eye fairy..."

Then he looked at the stunned expressions on the faces of all of us who were wondering what had gotten into him and he suddenly started laughing.

People watching can be a lot of fun.

Malena (1 ½) knows lots of good word opposites now. Up-down, on-off, in-out, open-shut. She was hilarious watching the rock climbers. She would say, "Up, up, up" as they scaled the cliff.

Then when they were descending, she would squeal a delighted, "Wheeeeeeee!"

Find joy in those around you.

We were in Kmart in Montana with Daddy pushing one cart and I another. Amanda (5) was in Daddy's cart. It became embarrassingly obvious that she was not used to the Montana hair "style". A very large man with a very full beard and long hair, clothed in flannel shirt, jeans, large belt buckle (you get the picture) passed by Daddy's cart. Amanda pointed directly at the man and started laughing (chortling, perhaps is a better description). It was obvious to the man that she found something about him highly amusing. Daddy was wishing there were some way to make a graceful exit unnoticed!

One should always meet life with a great deal of enthusiasm. The infamous "they" has said that life is about enjoying the journey. Here's a great example of finding joy in life.

> Amanda celebrated birthday number 3! What a fun day we had! We got to all do some bubble-blowing outside; we went out for ice cream cones. We played. We ate manicotti for dinner. We took the boys to Grandma's house and then Mommy, Daddy and Manda went to the park. There was a 15-foot high slide that Amanda loved the most. She must have gone down it 50 times or so and each time at the bottom she'd grin and say, "I wanna do it again!" before we could suggest something else. She really had fun!

Turn negatives in to positives.

> We playfully asked Amanda (6) if she would like a 'swift kick in the bum' for her birthday. She responded, "Will you wrap it up?"

Be proud of yourself!

> Patrik (7) lost two teeth! After losing his first one, he walked around for two days with his lower jaw jutting out and a silly grin on his face.

Enjoy the highlights--To the max!

Kevin and the boys have followed the NBA playoffs. Brayden (6) knew his team would win game 5 right from the very start. Patrik (8) and Kevin started getting mad at a few of their plays for a while there, but Brayden never wavered! Amanda (7) comes in to watch the most exciting parts (the commercials) then goes back to coloring or whatever she was doing. Funny, funny girl.

Some things are more important than sleep.

Derek (2 ½) usually asks to go to bed somewhere between 7:30 and 8:00. He is just so good about it. I put him down and generally don't hear a peep until morning. A few weeks ago, however, he was put in bed and he just started crying and wouldn't quit. I figured he was probably overtired because he hadn't gotten enough sleep the last few nights.

I decided to take him out of bed and just snuggle and rock him to sleep. So, I put on a good "chick flick" and settled in to rocking.

After a half an hour he was still wide eyed. Thinking I had other things I needed to do, I told Derek, "You need to close your eyes right now and try to go to sleep. If you don't, I will just put you back in bed."

After I said this, I started to concentrate on the movie again. A minute or two later, I looked down at Derek. I had to keep watching him because he was more entertaining than the movie at the moment. His eyes were closed as tightly as could be, but every few seconds he would open one or both eyes slightly and peer at the television. Then he would shut them ever so tightly again.

I don't know how long he would have kept this up, but I could only keep from chuckling for a few minutes. When he heard me, he looked up at me with serious, big, blue eyes, and then he resumed watching the TV. I sure couldn't fault him for trying to obey my "stern" rebuke. Needless to say, after that, I just decided to enjoy snuggling and the movie until he gave in to sleep of his own free will.

Be excited about prizes.

Sean turned 5. He got a birthday party this year. It was a dinosaur party. About a dozen kids came over and played pin the tail on the dinosaur and other dinosaur games. The big hit was the prize for the pin the tail on the dinosaur game. (Kevin had drawn a large stegosaurus on butcher paper which was given to the ecstatic winner.)

Yippee!

Each child gets a turn of the day at our house. This means that whoever has turn of the day gets to pick the video to watch, choose where to sit, etc. This is really helpful when problems occur. It happened to be Derek's (3) turn of the day on this day when he and Sean (5 ½) were sitting in the kitchen munching on a snack. My back was to them so when someone hiccupped, I remarked, "Somebody's got the hiccups!"

Derek proclaimed with a grin, "Yup, it's me. It's my turn of the day!"

Messes can be fun.

The kids insisted I write this down in the journal. They really got a kick out of it. Brayden (8) asked for some applesauce, so I told him, "Sure, go ahead."

He got out the container of applesauce and a plate. He decided to pour himself some applesauce. He proceeded to dump half the contents of the jar onto his plate and the table. He gave me a sheepish, slightly worried look and said, "Uh, Mom? I got too much."

Well, I figured I could either chide him about his mishap or do something silly since he already knew he did a dumb-dumb. So, I yelled urgently, "Kids! Come here, quickly! Brayden needs help!" They came on the double and I handed each one a spoon and told them to help Brayden. So, my gleeful children ate applesauce by the spoonful from plate and table.

The best things in life are the simple things.

Wynter (4 months) is funny. He has discovered his feet and just likes to lay there holding onto his feet and grinning.

Wynter's favorite toy is a Nerf dart that lost its suction end. He gnaws on it like crazy as its interior fills up with saliva. Then he takes and flicks it with his hand so that anyone within range gets a nice shower

~ Chapter 3

Don't Be Afraid to Stand Up for Yourself!

Kids don't know that they are "supposed to" be embarrassed, worry about what someone else might think, or worry about whether or not they are being politically or socially correct.

Sometimes my kids say exactly what I am thinking:

> Brayden (2) was disturbed in church by the volume of the organ at church on Sunday. Every time the organist started to play Brayden would holler, "Too loud, 'kay?!"

I shouldn't be afraid to ask for what I am worth:

> Patrik (5) came to help Mom get some cleaning done after we made cookies. He cleaned the table off very nicely and got all the cookie dough off it. After I complimented him, he questioned me in a very business-like manner, "Do you want to give me a penny or a nickel?"

How will you ever learn if you don't give it a go?

I love it when kids try out new words. Often the meaning doesn't unfold as they would wish. For instance, picture Sean (7) coming in to a dinner of split pea soup. With a look of complete revulsion on his face he says, "I can NOT resist eating that stuff!"

You should always tell it like you see it!

A favorite Uncle enjoyed trying to coerce Malena (2) into talking with him. One time he asked her to tell him who was a "nerd". Amanda, deciding to be silly, exclaimed, "Ooh! Ooh! Pick me!"

Malena didn't have to ponder about this long before pointing her fingers and proclaiming, "Two nerds!" (She was pointing at her Uncle and Amanda.)

Speak up so that you will get what you want...or at least as close as possible.

Five year old Malena is quick to pick up on what the rest of us say. Yesterday she told me she was hungry.

I told her, "Have some carrots."

She said, "No, I don't want carrots."

I simply replied, "Oh, well."

Then she says, "No, I want to know what my options are."

It is important to take a stand sometimes. It is amazing how kids can communicate even at a young age.

I went to get Brayden (11 months) up from bed this morning. Upon finding that he was soaked, I immediately put him down and went to get a change of clothes for him. Apparently this offended him because he just cried and cried. I got the new clothes and sat on the floor and held my arms out for him to come to me. Well, that little stinker has learned what "no" means. All he would do was cry harder and shake his head "no". I finally had to go to him and pick him up. (He forgave me quickly however.)

Don't let anyone make you do something you don't want to do.

Daddy was trying to teach the kids some Korean. He told them a pig was "tedji". Patrik (4) and Manda (3) both said, "tedji." Kevin asked Brayden if he could say it. Brayden's (2) voice was loud and clear when he said, "No! I can't say 'tedji!'"

Children get older. Even when, or perhaps especially when, we aren't looking!

> Well, Sean (2 ½) doesn't want me to call him baby anymore. He says, "I not a baby. I bigger!"

Let them mature.

> I took Sean (2 ½) to the library with me. I went to the section of books for his age group. There were many nice picture books and board books I thought might interest him. I sat down on the floor and motioned for him to join me. "Come pick out some books you want to check out," I said.
>
> He came over to me, folded his arms and turned up his face. Indignantly he told me, "I don't want those books! Those are baby books! I'm not a baby. I a big boy!"
>
> With that he turned and marched over several aisles, looked purposefully through some books and pulled one out, saying, "I want this one." It was an art and craft book geared toward about 7 to 10 year olds.

If you know you are right, stick by your guns!

> Brayden (5 ½) spelled words on his own again. He wrote the word "chrees". Saying it out loud, I understood what it meant. It sounds exactly the way he says trees. I tried to

explain the way the word should actually be spelled. Brayden was adamant. He was so obviously correct in his own mind that he could not be convinced. Later as we were reading together, Brayden came across the word trees three different times. Each time he was completely astonished to see that they had spelled the word wrong. Never once thinking he himself could be wrong.

Kids are always quicker than you think.

I ran a very quick errand to my Mom's store while I left Patrik (9) in charge at home. Thinking I would be smart and test the kids to see if they remembered what to tell people on the phone, I had Mom's employee call the house and ask for me.

She did this and Amanda (8), who answered the phone, told her I wasn't home and yes, she knew where I went. When I got home I thought I better make a few corrections and stress how important it is to not let on that they are home alone.

I asked if anyone had called while I was gone. I specifically asked if Amanda told them I was not home. Amanda got one of those looks on her face that says, "Uh oh, I got caught". It lasted for just a split second, after which she quickly told me "But Mom, it was just the lady from Mormor's store!"

The store worker did not identify herself when she called and Amanda really hasn't been around her much, so I was pretty shocked to know that she recognized her voice!

Little people are people too.

Tonight Sean (5) was going to read a scripture story from his reader for us for our scriptures before bed. Because Derek (2 ½) was jabbering away, I told him, "Sean is reading a story to us, so be quiet."

Derek looked at me indignantly and replied, "So me!" (Translated: "So am I"). Indeed he was. He had a book about sharks that he was diligently pointing out things to his Dad.

The way things really are…

Malena (3) was wearing an outfit with the Diamondbacks logo on it. I told her that it was a good shirt to wear to a baseball game because it had the Diamondbacks on it. She gave me a very puzzled look, "No, it doesn't."

Then she tugged on the back of her shirt and tried to look at it in order to show me, and then she proclaimed, "See?" (Sure enough there was no diamond on the back of her shirt ☺)

~ Chapter 4

Thoughts on Pregnancy, Potty, Puberty, Growing Old & Other Similar Themes

It is always interesting to note the things children think about on the subject of pregnancy. For instance:

> Amanda (3 ½) likes to put her head on my tummy and listen to the baby and feel him moving. The baby was moving quite a bit for her and then became very still. Manda kept her head on my stomach anyway. I asked her if she thought the baby had decided to take a nap and stopped moving around. "No," she said very knowingly, "He's still splashing around."

Who can have babies?

> I told the kids about our coming baby and that the baby was in Mommy's tummy. Amanda (3) lifted her shirt to show me her tummy. Brayden (2) wanted to show his 'baby' too. He

opened his mouth wide. "See my baby?" he asked. "It's way down there."

Do you know where babies come from?

Brayden (2 ½) was helping Dad put the baby's cradle together. A piece was missing, so I asked Brayden if he wanted to go with Daddy (meaning to the store to get a part). Brayden said, "Yeah! Are we going to get the baby?"

What happens to you during pregnancy?

Being in my last month of pregnancy, Malena (5 ½) has been impressed with the size of my stomach. The other day, she said to me, "Mom, you're probably going to get bigger than the fridge."

You're never alone.

I had been Christmas shopping and mentioned to the family that there had been an unusual amount of pregnant women at Walmart while I was there. Brayden (15) quipped, "Ooh! I bet it was difficult to navigate the aisles!"

The bathroom has always been a place where humor and little ones go hand in hand. For instance, why have a switch if you don't use it regularly?

Patrik (3) had just gone to the potty. I looked over at the bathroom and it looked like he was having trouble turning off the light. I went over there and the fan was on. I said, "Patrik what did you turn the fan on for?"

He put both hands on his hips and sternly explained to me, "Mommy, I had to grind up the poop."

When ya gotta go, ya gotta go.

Here's one Daddy found funny... [Kevin's words]..."The other day I was helping Brayden (2 ½) go to the bathroom. I had to wipe his bum, (which isn't very pleasant). As I was just about done Brayden said, "Doesn't say yuck?"

I guess I must say "yuck" most of the time that I wipe his bum and he just thought that saying "yuck" must be part of wiping his bum.

The next time I made sure I said "yuck" and Brayden said, "Daddy says yuck!"

If you don't ask, you might live in wonder for a long time.

Brayden (6) opened the door when Kevin was in the bathroom shaving and asked, "Does that hair tickle your pits?"

How do you like your shower?

Derek (6) asked me this unusual question the other day—"Does Dad wear a jock when he takes a shower?"

Derek then insisted that Dad told him he did.

Where do they come up with these things??

The sun will come out tomorrow.

Malena (2) likes to pretend she is Annie. She sings "Tomorrow, Tomorrow, I love you. Tomorrow, you only day way!"

She is potty training right now and for some reason instead of saying she needs to go potty, she says "I pooping". So, the other day, she says "I pooping! No! I Annie! Annie pooping!"

Growing up is a natural thing, why get embarrassed?

A man and a boy are here putting in new windows today. Brayden, (7) as usual, is interested in handyman's work. He asked the boy many questions that the boy kindly answered. After a while, Brayden asked, "How old are you?"

The boy replied that he was 14. Brayden then commented, "Hmmm. Well it looks like you are growing a mustache."

The boy quickly became involved in a conversation with his adult employer. I imagine if I could have seen his face, it would have been beet red!

Sometimes bad manners lead to enlightening conversations.

> Someone "tooted" at the dinner table and claimed he couldn't stop it from happening. I told him he would never get married with that kind of thinking. Patrik (15) chimed in at this time, "Well, Dad got married."
>
> I informed the kids that Dad never once did that in my presence before we got married. With a completely straight face, Patrik protested in an alarmed tone of voice, "Now that's false advertising!"

Getting older is just something that happens. It happens to every one of us. It can be interesting to see a child's take on the matter, however.

Ever wonder what makes a person old?

> Patrik (4) and I were reciting nursery rhymes together and I was very impressed at how well he remembered them. I said, "Wow, how do you remember all those?"
>
> He said, "Mommy, don't you remember them?"
>
> I said, "I do, but I'm old."
>
> This really tickled Patrik and he laughed really long and hard. When he could finally talk

again, he said to me, "But Mommy, you still have hair!"

And you can laugh about it or be upset. Choice is yours!

In church, Brayden (3) went up to an older fellow, made sure he had his full attention, and then observed, "Hey! You don't have any hair!"

Thankfully the man just chuckled and said he wished we could all be so forthright! Later he also told Kevin that that comment had just made his day.

Not only do kids picture "old" people to be bald, but they have other qualities as well.

Brayden (3 ½) tucked his upper and lower lips into his mouth, covering his teeth up. While in this state, he says, "Hey look Mom, I look like one of those old guys!"

If you are ancient, you are in good company.

We were talking to the kids about how we receive the Lord's word. We were trying to get them to say, "through the scriptures". Patrik (6) mentioned that we hear the words of the prophet on TV during conference time.

Kevin said, "What about Moses, Noah, and the old ancient prophets?"

Brayden (4) thought he knew another one, so he piped up saying, "Yeah! And Val!" (Val is a nice balding man in the bishopric that the kids love.)

At least growing old has some advantages.

Grandma said we must include this in the journal.

Grandma and Grandpa were visiting. Sean (3) informed his Grandpa that he was fat. Later on, something was said and Grandma asked if Daddy was the boss. Sean quickly interjected, "No, the fat guy is the boss!"

I learned how to invoke terror in to the heart of my daughter. (hee hee)

I'll admit. I have pulled about 7 or 8 gray hairs from my head in the last year and a half (I'm 39). Sadly, those light colored hairs show up well against my dark hair. What an awful thing those first few were. But, having gotten over the initial trauma, I have accepted the inevitable...I think.

So, the other day, I found one sticking straight up and I told Amanda (16) to yank it for me. She looked at me very sympathetically, but did the job while asking, "You are getting white hair already?"

Hilariously, her sympathy very quickly turned to one of horror as she had a new thought, "Will that happen to me when I am your age too??!!"

~ Chapter 5

Take a Risk, Try Something New & When in Doubt, Fake It

Occasionally you should really just let go and have a blast when given the opportunity!

> We left the kids with Grandma and Cousins for a few hours. I told Patrik (3) I was going bye-bye. He quickly turned to one cousin and said "My Mommy's going bye-bye, you want to have fun?'

You never know what might be really, really fun...

> Dad gave Patrik (5 ½), Amanda (4 ½) and Brayden (3 ½), a penny to throw in the wish pond. When asked what she wished for, Amanda said, "I wished to swim in the wish pond."

You can learn from other people's experience...or not.

At the dinner table tonight, Sean (13) became impatient with something I had said and slammed his hand down. His hand hit the end of his fork, catapulting it into the air and smacking him in the head. This got a chuckle and a "serves you right" type of response.

What happened next really had us rolling in the aisles, though, as we watched Derek (10) mimic Sean. His 3-pronged fork caught him square on the nose. Someone said, "It's a good thing that fork didn't have only 2 prongs, or you would have poked both your eyes!"

We were all laughing so hard. Derek had tears come to his eyes. I believe he realized you can learn from other people's dumb mistakes, or you can try it out for yourself!

Kids believe they can do anything. We should follow their example and go for it all. Even if we miss the target, we might just get close!

Trying out new things is something that kids are always doing. They are always learning, discovering, trying something new.

Well, isn't that clever?

Patrik (2) learned how to do a front handspring. He learned accidentally while doing somersaults. He doesn't land on his feet, however.

You never know unless you try.

Amanda (1) loves the word bubble. She learned to say it from seeing bubbles in one of the Mickey Mouse books we have and now she says it all the time. Not only does she love the word, but she also enjoys eating them by the handful in the tub!

It might be strange, but also enjoyable.

Manda (2) loves to wear a square red plastic bucket on her head for a hat. She leaves it on her head for a long time as she plays with other toys.

Make your own fun.

Sitting at the dinner table, Brayden (3) all of a sudden squinched his eyes up tight and left them closed for a long time. I finally asked him what he was doing. He exclaimed, "I'm making it dark!"

Get around however you can.

Sean (3 ½ months) can now roll over both ways, stick out his tongue, blow bubbles and has just discovered his toes. If I put him on his blanket with toys around him, he'll maneuver himself around to grab at the toys. He has no problem going around in circles. He loves to grip things with his little toes. He likes to move himself so he's in a position to kick and push his feet into the couch. A couple days ago I put Sean on his tummy in the middle of my bed and went to do something. I was gone less than a minute and when I returned he was at the edge of the bed. What he does is he digs his toes into the bed with his bum way up in the air and scoots forward on his face!

The joys of discovery...

Sean (4 ½ months) now sits up quite well, and has gotten up on all fours. In church on Sunday, he started banging Gumby toy on Daddy's shoulder. Ever since, he seems to have realized there's something to do with toys other than eat them! He loves banging them now, especially the noisy ones.

Try out new snacks.

The other day Derek (8 months) crawled over to where I keep my garlic. I saw him and finished typing a sentence before I went to grab him. In that time he had peeled himself a clove and bit off a few bites. Boy did he smell wonderful!!! The crazy thing is--He liked it!

Go on joy rides.

As Sean (4) was shaking his head vigorously back and forth he said, "Mom! I am making the whole house move!"

Put on your make-up before going out.

Malena (2) went to get her shoes because we were going somewhere. She came back a few minutes later and says, "Does my make-up look good right there?"

She was completely serious and I had to try hard not to laugh. She had found Amanda's cover-up and delicately applied some to her lips and also had painted several stripes across her forehead all the way up to her hairline. So, I simply explained that we don't use cover-up on our lips. Then I washed her off and got her some lip gloss for her lips.

She was fine with that.

Exercise is fun and necessary.

Derek (7) has turned into the jump-rope king! He has taken up jump-roping in the last week. When he holds his face just right he can jump backwards very quickly. Then if he changes facial positions, he can do "crossies". His record is 12 in a row so far. Each different trick he does requires different tongue positioning. It is really cute to watch. He has two speeds—fast and tangled!

There's nothing tastier.

> The other day Malena (3) requested "smackamoni and cheese"

There's a word for when someone doesn't treat you as they themselves would like to be treated.

> I just heard Malena (3) say to Derek (8), "You're a 'hickapret'!" I think she got that from hypocrite. Hee hee.

You know what you are saying even when no one else does, so when you are in doubt, you can fake it!

> Though he doesn't know all the words, Brayden (1) always chimes in when someone is being scolded. He points his finger at them and starts jabbering intently at them like a little chipmunk.

Improvisation often makes sense.

> Patrik (2) now sings, "Twinkle, twinkle little one star, how you doing way up there."

Why not try speaking in code so not everyone understands.

> The kids (at 4,3,2) think that the correct terminology for the word pizza is to say that it is "pizza hump". They must have derived that one from Pizza Hut commercials.

A new version can be more fun.

> The kids (at 4, 3, 2) like to say some of their favorite phrases along with the video they are watching. In "Aladdin", the Genie in the form of a bee is going out of control in a downward spiral. He says, "Mayday, Mayday!" as he is going down. The kids always join in, saying, "May-naise, May-naise!"

Combining words gets the point across.

> We were taking the kids to a matinee for a surprise and asked the kids to guess where we were going. Amanda's (6) first guess was, "To the videeator?"

Yum, yum!

> A Chevy commercial was on TV and, Derek (5), was not terribly impressed until they told the name of the vehicle they were advertising. He excitedly repeated what he had heard, "Mom! A Chevy Taco, a Chevy Taco!"

We get the meaning, if not the words.

> Brayden (10) straightened up the library books and announced, "I am going to show the other kids how I organized these. That way the books won't get all hitler-skitler."

I love this new song:

Malena's (2) first attempt at Head, Shoulders song goes like this, "Head, Shoulders, knees and toes, Lena's toes, Lena's toes."

~ Chapter 6

The Gospel and God According to Wee Ones

In Isaiah 11:6 it tells us that, "a little child shall lead them." That is sure a true statement! The kids always have interesting viewpoints on things from the scriptures.

The Book of Mormon tells the story of those who populated the Americas before Columbus came. (Yes, the Native American Indians.)

> We are reading Book of Mormon stories to the kids in the mornings. One morning we were talking about the Lamanites. I said they had dark skin. Patrik (2 ½) looked at me with big wondering blue eyes and asked, "Oh, they can't see?"

Always pray for the things that are in your heart.

> In his prayer last night, Patrik (3) said "Bless the animals in the zoo and bless we can go there and get some ice cream."

The Bishop is similar to a Pastor, only he is not paid.

We moved into our new ward. The Bishop and his counselor came over. Brayden (1 ½) and Amanda (2 ½) started saying, "hey, guys" over and over again.

Patrik (3 ½) corrected them saying, "They aren't guys, they're parents."

Pray for want you want most.

Daddy had been working long hours for a couple weeks. The kids really missed him. Amanda (2) said in her prayer one night, "Bless Daddy can come home sometimes."

God made us in a wonderful way.

I asked Brayden (2) why he was so smart. He said, "Cause, I like too."

In answer to the same question, Patrik (4) said, "Because that's the way God makes us."

People serve voluntarily; doing different things within the church, such as teach a Sunday School class. Stake Conference is a regional meeting.

Church is for convicts too… (Well, don't they need it?)

We had been to stake conference where they had released several people from serving in their callings. Somehow Brayden (5) got the wrong idea I could tell as he leaned over to me and animatedly whispered, "They escaped from jail?!"

There are lots of ways one can be "moved" by the Spirit.

Patrik (8) describes the way the Holy Ghost gives you a good feeling, in this manner: "It makes me feel like I could jump forever!"

Remember the Sabbath Day to keep it holy.

Today, Sunday, Sean (7) asked me if he could go outside. I said he could but to keep in mind that it is Sunday and playing ball was probably not his best choice for a Sabbath day activity. "Okay." he said.

I went out a few minutes later to check on Sean and Tanner. They were both out there, golf clubs in hand. I asked Sean if I hadn't just said that playing ball was probably not the best thing. He confidently responded, "But I am not using a ball. I'm just practicing my swing."

Somehow, I don't think he quite understood the point I was trying to get across.

God understands us.

Malena's (2) prayer the other day "Heavenly Father Bless ...unintelligible words... Thank you. Baseball fun. Golf fun. Amen."

Monday night is set aside as Family Home Evening (FHE). No other church activities are planned on that night.

Truly little children know more than they get credit for.

> Last night for FHE, we were talking about what to do in case there was a fire in the house. Brayden (13) had printed out an escape plan for our house that he had made. We talked about staying low, about breaking windows if needed, smoke, etc.
>
> Malena (3) sat in my lap and listened very intently. When the lesson was winding down to a close, Malena decided to speak. She said, "And, there are angels."
>
> We all readily agreed with her. "Well," she said, "Angels will help us to be safe."

Once a month is Fast Sunday. The money that would have been spent on those meals is given to charity. Young children aren't expected to fast. Little ones want to do what they see the grown-ups doing.

> It is fast Sunday today. Malena, at 5, isn't asked to participate in this. However, today when I asked her if she was ready for lunch, she replied, "I'm fasting lunch today."
>
> Derek (10) told her, "You don't have to fast."

She responded, "I want to get closer to Jesus and Heavenly Father. That is why I am fasting for lunch."

About an hour later, she determined that she would like to just have a "snack" before church.

And the interpretation thereof is...

We read tonight from Proverbs 13: 4 -- "The soul of the sluggard desireth, and hath nothing: but the soul of the diligent shall be made fat."

Sean (13) said, "I don't want to be fat!" We read again and discovered it is the soul that is to be fat, not the physical body.

Patrik (18) then quipped, "So, I will have a fat soul in a skinny body. At least I will be '<u>full</u>' of the Spirit."

It is astonishing how much we can learn about all things heavenly when presented with various ideas from kids.

The Lord makes great music.

Patrik (2 ½) saw a picture of Jesus with trumpeting angels. He said "Look mom, they all have doot-doos." Then he added "Except Jesus." (The kids like to take paper towel rolls and say doot-doo into them like a horn.)

God gives great gifts.

> We have tried to teach Patrik (2 ½) that everything we have the Lord has given us. Explaining to us about Christmas time, Patrik says "It's Jesus birthday," but he also says, "Jesus gives lots of presents to Santa Claus and Santa Claus gives us the presents."

The Lord's goodness knows no bounds.

> I was picking carrots with Patrik (5). He was slightly overwhelmed with the amount of carrots I was giving him to hold. He said, "Mom, Jesus sure is giving us lots of carrots!"

You should always look for the Lord's hand in your life.

> We went to see an Uncle off at the Missionary Training Center. They had an overhead projector on which they switched back and forth two different messages to read while waiting for the program to start. When they changed it one time, Brayden (4) said to Dad, "See that Dad? It moved."
>
> Then he exclaimed, "I saw a hand!"
>
> He thought for a bit, then asked, "Was it Jesus?"

You should always have Godly thoughts in mind.

The other day, Patrik (7) answered the phone in this manner "Dear Heavenly…Oh, uh, Hello."

God can do anything.

Sean (4) was chattering at me while I was busy in the kitchen. One of the questions he came up with was "Is God bigger than Dad?"

I answered that I didn't know but I supposed God probably was bigger.

Sean says, "Yeah, I know He is because He can jump higher than Dad. Dad can probably only jump over Morfar. God can jump all the way up to Heaven. Nobody else can jump farther than this world. 'Cept Jesus. He can jump up to Heaven too."

(Dad is 5'9". Morfar is 5'11")

You don't have to be lonely.

Derek (5 ½) decided to eat lunch out on the trampoline. Sean (8), upon seeing Derek out there by himself, called through the open window, "Are you lonely Derek?"

"No", Derek responded. Then he hollered back, "Do you want to know why I am not lonely?"

Sean agreed, "Sure!"

The jubilant voice came back, "'Cause God is with me!"

God is just like us...

We were reading scriptures as a family the other day and I was helping Derek (6) with a few words. I would just whisper to him words that he wasn't getting right away to speed up the process. The scripture was talking about the fact that Heavenly Father has a body. After I whispered the word "body", I realized that you really can't whisper a "b" sound because I heard him say, "Even a potty". The funny thing was, it seemed to make perfect sense to him that God would have a potty.

God understands our trials.

Yesterday Malena (2) chronicled this prayer to her Heavenly Father. "Heavenly Father, we can go to Libby's house. And, and, and a ball hit me on my cheek. And amen."

It is good to be in the right place.

Today at church, Malena (2 ½) had a little play cell phone that she was playing with pretty quietly. She "talked" to various people on the phone. Then her eyes lit up as she looked up at her Dad and exclaimed, "Jesus is calling!"

Daddy asked her what he was saying. Lena said he told her to be in church.

Jesus did everyday things.

Malena (3) had to "read" a scripture verse as we were all taking turns today. She "read", "Jesus went to the farm and then He went to the temple, but He didn't want to be there, so He went out."

What is Jesus like?

Tonight for family home evening I prepared a short lesson to help us all share some of our testimonies with each other. I asked Malena what she believed. Malena (3 ½) said, "I believe in Jesus."

I questioned, "How do you know He is real?"

And Malena replied, "Because He has bones!"

Sometimes you just have to do things because it is the right thing to do.

I had asked Malena (3 ½) to clean her room in the morning. She didn't do it. Later that afternoon she came and told me, "Sometimes I don't want to clean my room. But, I should do what Jesus wants me to do. So, I will go clean my room." She did go get started on it then.

She got some of it done before she got distracted.

A good question...

I was reading about the Garden of Gethsemane to Lena (4) last night. She asked, "Why did Jesus have to pray?" And then to make sure I knew why she wondered, she added, "He is the Savior." I thought that was pretty deep thinking for a four year old.

The resurrection made simple.

Yesterday I read to Lena (4 ½) the story of the resurrection of Jesus. After He was resurrected, He went to see His disciples. Malena says, "Oh, but they don't get to come alive again."

So, I just simply explained that everyone will be resurrected, it just won't happen quite as quickly as it did for Jesus. Her question then was, "So, will they be resurrected in 4 days or 5?"

Learn to explain yourself well.

We read the story in the scriptures about casting stones at the sinner. I asked Derek (9) if he understood what was going on in the story. "Not really." he said.

I explained the story to him, ending with that Jesus said that whoever was without sin would cast the first stone. Then I questioned him, "So, after saying that, who is going to throw a stone at her?"

Thinking he would quickly say "no one", I was surprised when it took Derek a moment to respond. When he did reply, it was with a quizzical look on his face. "Jesus?" he said.

~ Chapter 7

Watch What You Say...Little People are Listening

It's always amazing to hear my own words spilling from my children's lips.

> Children do learn the most from their parents' example. Brayden (2) had taken a magnet off the fridge causing some papers to fall down. Patrik (4) went over to him, let out a deep sigh and said, "Brayden, I am trying to be patient with you. I am getting really frustrated. I don't know what to do. Now, let's put these back up and not do this again, okay?"
>
> Seems to me I have heard those words before.

There are certainly some unnecessary words in the English language.

> I forgot to do something that needed to be done and I said, "dang it!"

Brayden (2) looked at me inquiringly and asked, "What's dang it for?"

Kids pick up on even little phrases we say.

Amanda (3) woke up from a nap and asked, "Did Daddy take-off?" I think she has heard her Dad say that a few times!

That ol' spelling trick doesn't always work!

Grandma and I were discussing Sean's (2) birthday and I said she could just get him a teeny P-O-O-H (I spelled it out). Right then Sean jumped into the conversation with, "Whatdja say mom? P-O-O-H?"

I guess we forget kids hear more than we realize.

Kids take things quite literally.

We took the kids to the circus. Prices were rather high for all the extra activities. So, when I saw a child break a balloon shortly after purchasing it, I remarked, "Well, there went two dollars."

Shortly after saying this, I looked over at Amanda (8) who was groveling in the dirt under the bleacher. "What are you doing?" I asked.

She replied, as if stating the obvious, "I am looking for the two dollars!"

Everyone should help out.

The other day, Malena (2 ½) got on a stool so she could watch me wash some dishes. She asked if she could hold a sponge she saw. Then she decided she wanted the washrag and another sponge. Once she had all these, she started to scrub at the counter. She kept at it for quite some time.

Brayden (13) happened by, so she asked him, "Bubba, do you want to help me?"

Brayden declined saying, "No thanks, I'm fine." He then proceeded to exit the kitchen.

He only got a few steps from the kitchen before he heard Malena's stern rebuke, "You didn't even do anything to help!"

Just because kids don't say a lot of big words, doesn't mean they don't understand them.

Malena (3) was being a silly girl and Grandma told her so. Grandma questioned, "Where do you get your silliness from? Is it from your Dad?"

Malena was certain that wasn't it. She put one little finger up to tap on her cheek as she thought. Then she said, "No, no, it is from my...my imagination." (It actually came out sounding something like immanation, but she knew exactly what word she wanted.) Not too bad, huh? A five syllable word coming out of a three year old! Boy they pay attention to what goes on around them, don't they?

Little ones have memories like elephants.

One day, we needed the stud finder to hang some pictures on the wall. Kevin had brought it to his office and forgotten to bring it home. The next day, I asked him if he had brought it home. He had forgotten.

A couple of days later I walked into the house around dinnertime. Malena (2 ½) came running up to her Daddy, neglected to say "hi" or give him a kiss. Instead, she asked, "Dad, did you bring the stud finder?" She doesn't even know what a stud is. Then again...maybe she does!

~ Chapter 8

Appreciate and Know the World Around You

The wonderful world of kids shows us a lot of fun things that we otherwise wouldn't know about or notice.

You can hear a lot of fascinating things if you just pay attention.

> Today Amanda (2) heard a chain saw and said "Cow, Mommy, hear it?" I guess to her it sounded like a prolonged moooooooo.

Sleep should not prevent you from being in touch with your world.

> Last night I was trying to rock Brayden (1 ½) to sleep and he started singing the teeter-totter song to me. (Teeter-totter, bread and water wash your face in dirty water.) I had to laugh, because that song is not exactly a lullaby!
>
> Then a bit later as he was drifting off to sleep, my stomach growled a bit. Brayden opened his mouth long enough to say "burp" then fell right

back to sleep. He is always very cognizant of what is going on around him.

Make sure to tell your hair dresser the style you really want.

Yesterday we were up at Grandma's house and got the kids' hair cut. Grandma cut a lot of hair from Brayden's (2) head. It was really short and cute. We gave Brayden the mirror to look at so he could see how cute his new haircut was. He looked in the mirror, made a really inquisitive face and said "Who dat in dere?"

Stick with whoever is in charge!

Grandma was watching the kids at her office. She left the room momentarily and three agents stayed in the room. They then left also. Patrik (6) came out to find Grandma. He told her, "Grandma, the grown-ups left us all alone."

There are many amazing things in nature.

Today we were outside playing and Amanda (2) came up to me and said "Pider, Mommy, look Mommy, Pider!" She was holding up a wiggling, squirming bug between her two little fingers. The so-called spider turned out to be an earwig. I wonder how she managed to pick the crawling insect up?!

God has provided many beautiful things for us to look at.

> Brayden (1) loves the flowers outside. He squats and points and with large wide eyes he says, "ooh!" over and over again.

Even commonplace things can be extraordinary.

> I was putting together the Swedish angel chimes for Christmas time. Before I had it completely put together, it picked up some wind and started dinging a bit. Brayden's (2 ½) big blue eyes held astonishment as he breathed "Oh! It's like magic!"

~ Chapter 9

Use Your Imagination

This is one place that children really shine. They imagine exciting ways to play, stories, games, everything. It is great!

Happy endings are awesome.

> Tonight Patrik (4) told Daddy the story of the three bears. It was really good too. At the very end he said, "She woke up because of the little bear's voice and was really scared. So she ran around and around and ran all the way home but she couldn't find it. So the bears came and helped her find it."

Shakespeare made up new words, why shouldn't I?

> We were outside playing and Amanda (3) came up to me and whispered something. Not sure I heard her right, I questioned, "What?"
>
> She repeated, "Erbie".

I said, "Erbie?"

She said, "Mmhmmn. It's spelled B H." She then ran off to play some more.

There's more than one way to get attention.

We were visiting with Grandma at her office. Brayden (2 ½) and Amanda (3 ½) started telling Grandma about recent 'owies'. Amanda said she "bonked on the sidewalk".

Grandma said, "That's awful!"

Brayden said he bonked on the sidewalk too. And a snake got him. Grandma laughed and said, "I think you're telling me a fairytale!"

Brayden looked hurt as he said to her, "Not a fairytale! It's awful!"

Parents don't always choose the best.

Brayden (almost 3) says baby's name is Soopy Dooby.

Make-up is a wonderful thing. I look so beautiful when I wear it.

I had just put my mascara on and Brayden (3) came to me and said, "Mommy, you got spiders on you eyes."

You can make a game out of just about anything.

> Sean (10 months) has figured how to shoot flippy-doodles on his own. What, you may ask, is a flippy-doodle? Flippy-doodles are soft, fuzzy, elastic ponytail holders. The kids launch flippy-doodles at our ceiling. The ceiling has this kind of bumpy texture to it and the flippy-doodles stick to it. When one flippy-doodle has stuck, the object of the game is to shoot it down with another flippy-doodle.

Are you ever too old to imagine things?

> Patrik (12 1/2) lost a molar the other day. He put the tooth in a cup for the tooth fairy as he has done since he began losing teeth. The following morning, he searched for his fairy funds only to find that his cup of tooth had been cleared from the table and found its way to the dishwasher.
>
> So, he took me aside and said, "Mom, just give me the quarter, okay?"
>
> I feigned shock that he would think to ask me for something the tooth fairy was supposed to give him. I commented, "What, you think I am the tooth fairy?"
>
> Patrik responded, "Well, I just can't imagine Dad in a tutu."

You never know what might be tasty!

> We were watching a movie last night for Patrik's birthday. Malena (2) crawled up into her Daddy's lap and licked his face. "I lick you!" she says. "I kitty. Meow. Meow."

Sometimes playing can just plumb tucker a body out.

> Today, Malena (2) took several of her babies and had each of them "go potty". After their successes, she would kiss them and offer them words of encouragement. When they were done going potty, she took them to go "sleeping night-night." She carefully lined them up on her pillow and tucked them in. After a bit I checked on her and discovered she had nestled right up next to them and was sound asleep herself! Too cute!

Everything's more fun with a friend.

> Malena (3) has an imaginary friend named Bobby Joe. (I think Sean (10) helped her make him up.) Today Malena decided to throw the ball to Bobby Joe. Then she told me about how he has a big huge ball. I asked her where she heard of Bobby Joe. She told me, "He was in my class at church teaching about God."

Creative writing can be both fun and entertaining.

> Malena (5) "wrote" a story on about 4 pages of notebook paper, both sides. She asked me to

"read" it to her, but I had her read it to me instead while I typed it up. Here it is in its entirety as she spoke it.

Once upon a time there was a Dad and he went to the golf course to go golf. Then he won the golf game. He is the golf course champion. And now he gets the golf course champion necklace. And then when his son came, Patrik, he said, "Did you win?"

And he said, "Yes."

And Dad said to his son Patrik, "I will give you a million dollars cuz I have that much money."

Patrik goes to the bank and gives some of the money to the guy and he says, "Thanks."

And Patrik says, "I have a million dollars. My Dad gave it to me." Then he went back in his car and drived back to his home.

And Dad said to his son Sean, "I won the whole thing of golf!"

Then Sean said, "Will you give me some of your money?"

And Dad said, "Yes."

And Marika said, "Why are you giving the kids money?"

"Oh, cuz they want it. Well anyways, we will give tithing to the bishop." And so they gave tithing to their bishop.

And then they went back to their seats and said to their kids, "Be quiet in church!" Cuz they were being really loud. Then Mom and Dad said that they were going on a date the next night.

And then it was the next night and they went out to Olive Garden and ate some salad and some other stuff. And then they went to the store to buy stuff. And then they went to Mom's Mom and Dad. And they were just visiting them. Then they went back and said, "We love you" to their kids. And so they lived more each day. And they had a birthday next day.

And so, they came along to this bank and they had all their money in their bank. Sooooo, Dad went to a golf course the next day and he said to his kids, "We are going to the golf course", but not to Malena cuz she wasn't old enough. And so they went without their Mom or sister, Malena.

(And here is a picture I drew).

And so they went and said, "This is a sunny day."

So Amanda and Patrik said to Dad, "Well, why are we here anyway?"

"To go golfing." So they went on to the golf course and so they golfed and golfed and golfed and golfed and golfed and golfed until they got as sweaty as they would want to be. So they went on to the parking lot and so they had to go home now cuz they were as sweaty as they wanted to be, and so they just went home and got a drink and said to Mom, "We love you Mom."

So they still did live in their cozy home and then came the Grandma and Grandpa and Mormor and Morfar. Dad's Dad and Dad's Mom and Mom's Dad and Mom's Mom. So all of them went shopping to go get some food for the kids. And they went to the store to buy some food. And they bought some candy for the kids too. Well, Mom we are going to live forever. So they lived forever. And they went. So they lived happily ever after. Love Mom and Dad.

That's All.

Using your imagination can help when you need to be extra resourceful.

Creativity comes in handy.

Amanda (3) peeled her celery stick and used one of the strings to pretend to tie her shoelaces on her little foot.

Logically speaking…

Tonight Sean (4) requested that I get him one of those "cold blankets". I figured out that it was a pillowcase that he could put his legs in.

There are ways to get out of being uncomfortable.

We got Derek's (1 ½) pajamas out to put on him after we read scriptures with the kids. While we were reading, Derek got down and, dragging his pajamas behind him, toddled down the hall.

After a while he came back. He had definitely been on a mission. In one hand he still held his pajamas; in the other hand his fist clenched a pair of scissors. He brought the clothing to Daddy and pointed to the toe portion. Then he handed Daddy the scissors. Then pointed back at the toe again.

In other words, "Daddy cut the footies out of these pajamas!"

Hold out for the best deal available!

Brayden (7) keeps losing his teeth in unusual ways. His tooth fell out onto the floor and we could not find it anywhere. We swept and combed the floor and found nothing. Another tooth came out in a tomato.

Brayden lost his third tooth in probably the craziest way yet. We were all at Daddy's cousin's house for dinner. Altogether there were about 50 relatives there. One Uncle discovered that Brayden had a tooth just hanging by a thread. He told Brayden he wanted to pull it out with some pliers. Brayden replied with an emphatic, "No!"

The uncle responded, "I'll give you a dollar if you'll let me."

You could see Brayden thinking that over. Another Uncle then chimed in with, "I'll give you a dollar if you'll let me watch."

Now Brayden was really mulling it over. Then a final Uncle had the clincher, "I'll give you another dollar if it draws blood."

Brayden didn't need to think anymore. His mouth just immediately dropped open as wide as could be.

He got his three dollars.

Decorate however you please.

We put up the Christmas tree tonight for FHE. It seems to take forever to get the branches all fixed how they should be, test the lights, string the lights, etc. While that was all getting done, I was sorting the ornaments into piles for the kids to hang.

Finally it was time to hang ornaments. Patrik (15) was still tinkering with the outside lights. But, I discovered that Malena (3 ½) was helping herself to his stash, so I told him he might want to go hang a few before Malena did all of his. After all the ornaments were hung, I took a look at the tree and thought it was a little sparsely decorated.

Scanning the room, I saw stockings hanging from various objects—my keyboard stand, the play stove, a chair, etc. The stockings were all loaded. Malena had managed to get the stockings all filled with ornaments and hung, all while drawing very little attention to herself. We sure got a good chuckle out of this.

However, this is actually not too surprising, because it is typical Malena behavior. She has a habit of picking up odds and ends from around the house and putting them in one of her many purses. She also loves to take rope and tie a whole chain of things together, or hook a bunch of hangers together. Sometimes you have to be on the look out around here because some of her creations turn in to booby traps!

A person can get outsmarted by a 1 year old.

We were at Mormor's house and Brayden (1 ½) wanted Mormor to help him shoot the ball in the basket. Mormor told him "I'm too short, I can't reach."

Brayden toddled away and came back with a small stool. He patted it saying, "Here Mormor, chair!"

Thinking about things in different ways can enliven your mind and enhance your imaginative skills.

Sometimes this involves drawing two common things together to make sense.

Kevin took Amanda (3 ½) with him shopping and she wanted to look at the toys before we left. There were a lot of horses on one shelf and Amanda was enjoying looking at them all. She spotted an Appaloosa and said, "Oh, this is a 'puppy-mation' horse!"

The bad and the ugly.

There was an unpleasant aroma and Manda (4) said, "Who tooted?"

Patrik (5) answered her by saying, "No one tooted, Manda, it's just morning breath."

Straighten up!

Patrik (5) was sick with fever and a tummy ache. He told Mom, "My body feels like it's all backwards."

It's a bird! It's a plane!

We went to watch the fireworks at the park. While waiting for them to start, an airplane flew overhead. Brayden (3) said, "Mom! That airplane had stars on it."

Patrik (5) apparently did not hear what Brayden said because when another plane flew by in the distance, Patrik exclaimed, "Those stars are flying!"

Planes, trains and automobiles.

Sean (2) told me today he didn't want to do potty-train he wanted to do diaper-train. Uh, that wouldn't be really helpful Seanie boy.

If it ain't broke, don't fix it.

Amanda (4) told me she broke her leg bone. So I looked and said she didn't break her bone. She said, "I broke my blood."

Wish for things that no one else would ever think of.

Brayden (3 ½) wants a toy Santa for Christmas.

Here's a good "play" on words.

We made lasagna and each of the kids asked for a "plain noodle" (a cold noodle that I don't put into the lasagna). Sean (2) interpreted the meaning of this differently than the other kids. He took his large noodle and plastered it to his forehead. He said to me excitedly, "I play noodle, Mom! I make hat! hee hee hee."

Make sure you use descriptive writing.

Brayden (5 ½) decided to write some words on his own. He wrote things like log, cat, slik, fun, etc. Then he decided he would write the word 'bear'. I told him that might be a bit difficult since it doesn't follow the rules.

I said, "I guess it depends on which kind of bear (thinking bear or bare) you want to write. Do you mean a growly bear kind of a bear?"

"No," came the reply. "I think I will just write a quiet one."

Always report your findings.

We were able to see a very low flying hot-air balloon today. It was probably no more than 15 feet above our neighbor's house as it passed by. The kids were all very impressed by it and of course had to report about it to Dad. Sean (3 ½) said the balloon was really, really huge and "it had a tiny guy in it."

Inside, Outside, Upside Down!

Sean (4) asked me, "Mom, would you inside out my pants?" His pants needed to be put right side in.

Get your measurements straight.

We have just moved and are staying in a 2 bedroom condo until we can move into a four bedroom home in a few months. We have driven by our 4 bedroom home to show the kids. Derek (3) calls the 4 bedroom home our "teeny house" and the 2 bedroom home our "big house". I guess if you look at it from his point of view, it is true. The condo is a couple stories high and a few condos wide, so judging by the outside, it is bigger!

Some things just look a lot alike.

I was at the grocery store the other day with Derek (3 ½) and Sean (6). I was lost in thought, so it took a minute for me to figure out what Sean had just excitedly blurted out. He said, "Look Mom! Tomato soup with Cheerios in it!"

I had to have a good chuckle when I turned around to see that he was pointing at some cans of Spaghettios.

~ Chapter 10

Be Friendly & Affectionate

Children don't have any qualms about other people. They know that every soul on this earth is a child of God and therefore, no one person is better than anyone else.

People are usually interested in things you have to say.

> Kevin's friend came over. Normally our kids take a while to warm up to new people, but on this day they all were very talkative. Brayden (2) kept calling him "Guy".
>
> He would say, "Guy, look my picture."
>
> Or "Guy, I have a kitty, my bed."

And to think, now I can hardly get most of them to be quiet! This same child has continued to be friendly and has improved his social skills. (I am seeing a political career here.)

> Kevin took Brayden (5) with him to hit golf balls at the driving range. Some of his instructors were there. Brayden, with his charming ways,

won them over. "It's nice to meet you, Brayden."

With that, Brayden would reply, "It's nice to meet you, too." He was very polite to them all.

You don't need to speak the same language to communicate with others.

I was at the doctor's office with the 4 youngest the other day and a little Mexican girl, maybe two years old, came over to Sean (10), dropped a book in his lap and said something in Spanish. Laughter came from the little girl's parents as Sean quickly told the girl, "No hablo Espanol."

Then the little girl moved on to try Derek (8). The parents were further entertained when Derek gave his reply, pointing to Sean he said, "What he said." Anyway, it was pretty funny.

It is a good thing to share love and hugs and kisses. Sometimes you should even double your love.

Derek (4 ½) came to give me the usual morning hug and kiss. He then smiled up at me and said, "Mama, I love you."

I said, "I love you too."

Quick as a whip, Derek came back with, "I love you twice!" and grinned from ear to ear.

Brotherly love is a glorious thing. (Okay, and sisterly.)

Malena (newborn) entered the world with the sweetest chubby cheeks, but the rest of her is pretty skinny. Here is what her siblings had to say:

Derek (almost 5): When asked what he thought about Malena, Derek simply said, "It's heavy!"

A couple days after the birth, Derek told me that now Malena would be getting more kisses and hugs than I do. I am not so sure I like that deal. Derek also asked a million questions.

"How did she get out of your tummy? Where does the milk come from?", etc.

He also was amazed at her fingers. "Her pinky is only this big!"

Sean (7): This boy had been pretty adamant about not wanting to have anything to do with another sister. But, guess who is the most reluctant to let her go? Sean said, "Once you start holding her you just don't want to let go."

I would have to agree with that.

Sean also questioned shortly after the birth, "Mom, why are you still fat?"

Brayden (10): "I am so glad she is here!"

Amanda (11): "My wish finally came true!"

Patrik: I don't recall what Patrik said, but I know he is missing her now as he is at Scout camp all week. I am glad he got to see her before he left.

There's nothing like a good snuggle with dear old Dad.

Daddy was gone for nearly a week. Malena (1) missed her Daddy. When someone mentioned him, she went in search of him. I picked him up at the airport at 10:00 at night, so she was already asleep for the night when we arrived at home. In the morning, she awakened at about 5:45. She seemed like she would go back to sleep again and I knew I wanted to, so, after nursing her, I laid her down in bed beside me. She stirred slightly as I did so and her eyes half opened. This was enough for her to catch a glimpse of another body in the bed. Her eyes flew open with excitement and she looked to me for confirmation, "Dida?" she questioned (means Daddy).

I acknowledged her by saying, "I was afraid of that", meaning that I saw her catch a glimpse of Dad and thought it might mean no more sleep for me! How could one resist that, though? She turned back to her Daddy and climbed into his arms for a good ten minutes of hugging and snuggling, hardly moving a muscle.

Kisses.

Kevin told the boys that I had told him something that made him want to come home early. (He was being sarcastic because I had actually told him to come home and solve my problems.)

So the boys decided to guess what it was. Someone volunteered, "She was gonna feed you!"

Kevin said, "No, but that's a pretty good one."

Brayden (12) said he knew what it was, "She was gonna kiss you and feed you."

Kevin thought that would work, but Sean (9) had a different opinion. He exclaimed, "That's sick! That is just sick!!"

~ Chapter 11

Learn Things, Ask Questions & Know the Reasons for Things!

Letters are fascinating.

> Whenever Amanda (2) sees letters she says excitedly "Mom! B!"

They start young...

> We were with Grandma and Grandpa leaving the parking lot of Stop & Shop. Patrik (3 ½) said he saw a lot of letters. Daddy asked what letters he saw and before Patrik could answer, Brayden's (1 ½) voice came quickly from the back seat, "O P!" We all laughed because he actually was right. Loving the attention, Brayden kept repeating "O P" and laughing at himself to make us keep laughing. Grandma was laughing so hard she nearly slid out of her seat.

Some things are important to take note of.

Patrik (4) learned from the "Robin Hood" video that snakes don't walk, they "sniggle".

Foreign language studies can be started at an early age.

I told Patrik (4) I needed some cooperation. He said he didn't know that word. So, I explained what it meant. Patrik emphatically exclaimed, "No, Mom, I mean is it Korean?"

I said, "No, it's not".

Knowingly he replied, "Then it's Swedish, huh, Mom."

As parents, you can never have too much information.

Mom and Dad have started to attend a parenting class on Sunday nights. Patrik (5 ½) said of this, "That's good because you are good parents sometimes and other times not."

So much for "Keeping up with the Joneses".

They have sitters for the kids while the parents attend class. When we arrived, Amanda (4 ½) commented, "There's not too much people here."

Patrik (5 ½) quickly told her the reason, saying, "That's because all the other people already know how to be good parents!"

Observation is a key to learning.

> I was going to play "Cooties" with the kids. Sean (8 months) sat in my lap and watched intently for 5 minutes. Then, deciding he had the game figured out, he picked up a part of my cootie and threw it on the board. He did this a couple of times; apparently thinking the object of the game was to throw things onto the game board. I decided to let him roll the dice when it was my turn. Every time I gave him the dice, he threw it straight to the board as soon as I told him, "Throw it!" He sat doing this the whole game, waiting patiently for his next turn. We played for 45 minutes.

Where is the best place to live?

> I was teaching the kids about a few different states. Apparently Patrik (6) was impressed with Connecticut because he said to me, "Well, Mom, after we get tired of living in Arizona, maybe we can move to Connecticut!"

Copying is learning

> Sean (2 ½) has entered the "why" stage. "Mommy, why you doing that coloring?"
>
> "Because I am writing a letter to my brother."
>
> "Why you writing letters to him?"

"Because I thought he might like a letter from me."

"Oh," he says very seriously, "I like letters too."

So I had to let him make some letters on my paper, too.

Try it out. You might be right.

Patrik (7) was telling me about someone the other day and he said that this person was a midget. I really didn't understand why he thought that, so I suggested that it might be another word he really meant. Then he said, "Oh yeah, I mean a comedian. I always get comedian and midget mixed up." (Sure, I see the connection).

Ask and investigate.

Brayden (6) forever wants to know how things work.

How does the TV work?

How do you make a video tape?

What makes a rocket fly?

Yesterday he lifted the lid from the keyboard on the piano partway and was able to see inside. He was so thrilled that he excitedly called to the others so they could come see how the piano works when you play the keys.

Oops!

Sean (6) was spelling some words out to me in sign language. He would hold up a hand sign and say, "what's that?" I would tell him and we spelled out things like 'let', and 'pop'.

Then Derek (3 ½) held up a hand sign and said, "What's that?" I looked at his little hand and only one finger was extended. I'll let you guess which one!

You can tackle even those tough assignments!

For school, Brayden (10 ½) has been using a book that has a reading assignment and then questions to answer after it. He came to me upon completion of the assignment and informed me, "I think Amanda would do better with this assignment than I would."

I wondered why he would say that. As it turned out, the assignment included much talk of, "stuff about girl's hair and other stuff."

"But," he said, "I think I figured it out all right."

Sure enough he had. He even described one of the girls with "curls about her head".

Liven up the dinner table discussions! Debates can be fun and educational.

Brayden (11) had discovered on a field trip with his scout troop that glass is a slow moving liquid. He shared this information with the rest of us. Patrik (13) would not believe a word of it. I told Patrik if he wanted to say that, he needed to have some evidence to back up his opinion.

Not too much later, Patrik reported at the dinner table that he had found a website supporting his claim. Brayden argued back, spouting off nice scientific words like molecules, atoms, etc. Patrik then did likewise with the information he had gained.

It finally got to the point where they kept repeating themselves. I told them if they wanted to argue this further, they would need to each get some more evidence to support themselves. (Patrik of course informed me they were debating, not arguing.)

Sean (8) chimed in to say that they could call Morfar. I said that they could use him for a reference, but how did they know whose side he would support.

Eventually, it dawned on me that this could qualify for the "intelligent conversation at the dinner table" that my mother always longed for. So, I couldn't resist giving them a call. We got Morfar's opinion which seemed to please both boys and hopefully Mormor and Morfar got a good chuckle!

Why not?!

Today I gave Derek (7) a reading assignment in the book "Frog and Toad Are Friends". He was to read aloud chapters 1 & 2. I was listening to him while doing other things in the kitchen. After a while I looked over at him. He was reading very proficiently, but something was unusual. He had the book upside down! I chuckled and asked, "Derek, why are you reading with the book upside down?"

He grinned back at me and stated, "Because I can." I suppose that is a good enough reason.

There's more than one meaning to a lot of words.

A few days ago, Derek (7 ½) and I were doing a science lesson that talked about animals that can camouflage themselves. He asked what camouflage was and I explained by mentioning his shorts that he has that are army camouflage. He said, "Oh, and my shirt too."

I didn't think he had a camouflage shirt and said as much. He responded by saying that he did indeed have a camouflage shirt that was blue with stripes. I just let it go at that.

Then a few days later, Derek came out with his "camouflage" shirt on and said, "See, Mom? This would be really good to hide in the water." Well, true enough. The shirt was varying shades of blue and white stripes. I suppose water can have those same colors.

Some lessons never end.

I am in the middle of Derek's (8 ½) science lesson on friction. It appears to be a never-ending loop. In an effort to get him to understand that shoes have built in friction, I am supposed to ask Derek if he has ever looked at the bottom of his shoes. "Yes", he says.

Then I should ask what the bottoms of the shoes look like. "Dirty", he says.

So, thinking to clear things up, I say, "If the shoes were clean, what do they look like?"

"Brand new!" comes the triumphant response.

I say, "No, I mean what is on the bottom of your shoes?" I should have seen it coming, but didn't.

His response? "Dirt!"

AAARGH! Okay, try again.

Some good ideas don't pan out.

The other day in history, I was trying to tell Derek (8 ½) a good way to remember the holy book of the Muslims. So, I told him he could remember it because Qaran sounds like crayon. He thought that sounded like a good way to remember.

The next day I quizzed him. I asked, "What is the holy book of the Islamic religion?"

He was quick with his response, "Crayola!"

Learning takes lots of time.

Malena (3) told me yesterday that she didn't like the movie she had watched. (It was a movie about big machinery that was supposed to be educational for kids.) She said it had buildings falling down in it. Then she left the room, but she came back about 30 seconds later and added, rather indignantly, "And it was only half a...a...a... half a hour!"

If you don't learn, you'll be sorry.

In the course of telling Daddy about her day, Malena (3) was remorseful when she said, "I didn't do all of my school work. I didn't do three of my books. So I am grounded."

Live and learn.

Derek (9) and I did a little research on Sir Christopher Wren via the internet, just for fun. He found the man to be a fascinating individual. At dinnertime, I asked Derek to tell everyone what Sir Christopher Wren is most famous for.

One could not help but laugh as he spluttered forth his exuberant response, "St. Paul's John!" He knew it was supposed to be "Cathedral" that he said, but for some reason his brain didn't connect with his voice box. He didn't realize why what he had said was funny.

Advertising jingles work! Thank goodness this particular jingle was accurate.

I was giving Malena (5) her spelling test today. The first word was "kiss". She debated about whether it should be a "K" or a "C" to start with. Suddenly her eyes brightened. "I know!" she said. Then she began to sing, "Every kiss begins with Kay."

What's in a name?

> Malena (5) tried to remember the word immigrant when we were doing a history lesson today. She said those people were called "nibbits".

Children are never hesitant to get things figured out. They will ask questions, make statements, guess and any number of other methods to arrive at a conclusion.

If something happens once, it is bound to happen again.

> We are living with Mormor and Morfar right now. One morning Morfar had to try and catch a cow that was on the loose in his yard. The next morning Patrik and Mormor were alone in the kitchen. Patrik conversed with Mormor with a two-year-old's zeal. "Brayden sleeping downstairs. Manda sleeping too. Mommy taking a shower. Morfar having a cow?"

Kids are pretty quick to figure out what is going on around them.

> You can tell that Patrik (2 ½) realizes we are not wealthy when he asks about nearly everything that we have "Oh, Mormor bought this?"

Be sure to know what is expected of you.

> Daddy was scolding Patrik (3) for hurting baby Brayden (11 months) again by saying, "How many

times do I have to tell you not to hurt the baby?"

Patrik said, "15".

Sometimes things that seemed clear to me become less clear when questioned by my children.

Kevin was working in the garden when he informed Patrik (4) that he was thinning the carrots. "Why do we want the carrots to be skinny?" asked Patrik.

Make sure things are in the right place.

Patrik (6) had a swollen bump on his foot and decided to tell Brayden about it. He said, "Brayden, I have a bump on my foot, that isn't supposed to be there."

Brayden (4) asked, "Where is it supposed to be?"

Life comes in stages.

Sometimes it is very humorous to listen in on the kids' conversations. Brayden (5 ½) and Sean (2 ½) were talking. Sean seemed to be aggravating Brayden with his questions. Brayden said, "Sean, you are in the 'Why' stage. You keep asking me why."

After thinking about it for a minute, he added, "I am still in the 'Why' stage too."

Sean concurred "Yeah, you are and me."

You can never ask too many questions. There may, however, be a limit as to how many you can listen to!

I am so exhausted right now I could probably fall asleep in front of this computer. I just got back from the library with Sean (3). How many questions do you think one boy can cram into a 5 minute car ride? I don't know; I lost track.

These are all actual questions he posed on the way to the library.

How far is it to the library?
How do we get there?
Where is the library?
Why do we want to go to the library?
Why is the library there?
Why can't they have the library back there?
Do we go straight, straight and then turn?
Why can't we turn first and then straight?
What time is it?
When will we get there?
Are we going to get lots of books?

Those are just the library-related questions and I quite possibly missed a few.

Where's the moon?
Why did the moon go back there?
What are those things?

(What color are they, Sean?)
They are just exakly that color, actually.
(Oh, are you talking about the light posts?)
Yeah, why are they light posts?
Why are there lights on?
Are we going to get strawberries?
When are we going to get strawberries?
Why are we following that guy?
What is that guy doing?
Is that guy going to get raspberries?
Why do we need to go this way?
When are we going to turn?
Mom, I thought we were going to turn. When are you going to turn? You missed it, Mom. We need to turn.
What does that say?
(Walgreens)
Are we getting strawberries there?
(No)
Why not?
(Because it is not a grocery store)
Why is it not a grocery store?.........

Sometimes you just have to know about stuff!

Today Brayden (6 ½) asked me this, "Do they write their numbers backward on the other side of the world?"

In life, there are good guys and bad guys. Be sure to know what each is about.

Amanda (8) wanted to know who was winning the basketball game. I told her we were up by 10. She said, "What are the bad guys up to?"

It's all in the pronunciation.

Sean (4 ½) and Derek (2) were playing basketball. Every once in a while, Sean would say, "Oh! It is out of bounce. Okay, Derek we have to throw up."

Grown-ups do really silly things sometimes.

Brayden (8) came into the kitchen wondering what I was doing. I said I was dishing up pineapple-upside-down cake. He inquired, "Why, did you drop it?"

Why did I never think to wonder about something like this?

Out of the blue, Malena (2 ½) came up and asked me, "Mom, do you know the muffin man?"

There's more than one way to look at things.

The other day I had cut up a bunch of veggies, including cabbage and put it in a bowl. I then transferred the veggies to my preheated frying pan so we could have stir fry for dinner. Malena (4) looked half puzzled, half shocked when she asked, "Mom! Why are you cooking the salad?"

Some things aren't what you think they are.

Derek (11) came to me with a plastic container that he had taken from the fridge. He questioned, "What's this?

I said, "It is evaporated milk."

Derek's response? A very puzzled look. Evidently my answer did not make any sense to him when he pondered the meaning of evaporated.

Stuff happens. Do you know why, though? It is always good to know the reasons, like in this example.

Mommy got a bad sunburn. Patrik (3) looked at my face and said "Mommy, you got warm!"

Know what you inherit.

I asked Brayden (2) why he talked so much. His answer was very serious, "because.....Grandpa."

Know what you are eating!

Amanda (4) was playing with one black Barbie and one white Barbie. They were talking to each other and the black one says, "Do you eat chocolate?"

The white one says, "No, we don't."

The black one then responds "Well, we eat lots of chocolate at our house!"

Know what you are drinking!

Kevin and I went to a fireside at the church where they had some of the young men and women babysitting for us. When it came time to collect the kids, Brayden (4) was sitting amongst some of the young men. They said they thought he had the best behavior of all the kids there. They had asked him this question, "Are you the most popular?"

He thought a minute before responding, "I don't drink pop."

~ Chapter 12

Logic & Important Facts

It depends on how you look at things...

> Patrik (3) saw the mailman come and go. He told his Daddy, "The mailman doesn't have a very good car."
>
> Mommy asked him why it wasn't good. Patrik's answer was very logical. "Because it doesn't have doors. Other ones have doors."
>
> Yup, 'tis true.

I just don't get this next one. How did he know that?

> Patrik (3) was crying out one night. I went in to see what was wrong before he awakened the other two. Well, Patrik was sound asleep as he was talking, but Brayden (1) was standing up in bed. The next morning when I got Patrik up I asked him if he had slept well. He said, "Yeah, but you didn't, you were up with Brayden."

Some things just have a logical conclusion.

In church we sat on the front row. Amanda (2) loudly observed as she pointed to the chorister, "That guy not have hair!"

Patrik (3) was quick with the explanation "That's because he's older."

Some things are not meant for everyone.

The kids were having yogurt for breakfast. Patrik (4) said, "This is boy yogurt. Brayden has some and I have some. And Amanda has some. Why did you give Manda 'boy yogurt'?" After much deliberation, Daddy figured out the problem. The yogurt was Boysenberry flavored.

How does a person drive fast?

Driving along the road, I wanted to pass a slowpoke. I said, "Come on, Bucko!"

Patrik (4) said, "Mommy how come he's going slow?"

I said, "Because he doesn't know how to put the pedal to the metal."

"Oh," Patrik said thoughtfully. "Is that because his legs aren't long enough, so he can't go fast?"

What do you know about gardening?

Kevin was watering the lawn and flowers. When I told Brayden (3) this, he knowingly said, "Oh! We want our grass and flowers to be clean, do we." (All 3 kids always say, "do we" instead of "don't we". They also say something that sounds like "were" instead of "our".)

Moms don't know everything.

I was referring to Sean (1 month) as I said, "Uh oh, spit-up."

Brayden (3) started chuckling and said, "He didn't spit up, Mom."

I wondered, "What did he do?"

Brayden pointed out, "He spit down!"

A good time to go to church...

Amanda (4) asked if we are going to church today. "No, we are not." I replied.

"Well", Manda says, "It is sunny out today!" (Sunday)

Thoughts on waking up...

At 8:00 a.m. Patrik (6) came up out of bed. We asked if his alarm clock went off.

"No." he replied, "It went on! It woke me up!"

In case you were wondering...

Sean (4) said matter-of-factly, "The ditch man came".

"Oh really?" I responded.

"Uh-huh", was his reply.

"What did he do?" I asked.

As if stating the obvious, Sean said, "He put water in the ditch!"

There's a difference between big boys and babies.

Derek (2 ½) was putting together some board puzzles today. I had given him one with just five pieces and a regular one. As I watched him do the puzzle, I commented, "You really are a big boy. You can do those puzzles." He agreed with my evaluation and said he can't do the baby puzzles (ones with few pieces) because he is a big boy.

I told him I still wanted him to be my baby because if he weren't, then I wouldn't have one. "No," he said, "I a big boy."

Then perhaps trying to discourage me from feeling bad that he isn't my baby anymore, he said, “Dey tan scratch you nose.” (They (babies) can scratch your nose).

“That’s true”, I agreed.

“Yep, dey tan.” He responded.

There’s different ways to make meals palatable.

At a dinner of split pea soup, Derek (5) was happily sucking up the broth through a straw. Brayden (10) questioned him with disgust obvious in his tone of voice, “How can you drink that stuff?!”

Derek, wondering why his brother would ask such a silly question simply answered, “with a straw” as if stating what should be plain to see.

Use deductive reasoning whenever possible.

We have started doing what Leo Buscaglia did as a child (at least frequently if not always). Every time they would sit down to dinner as a family, each family member would tell something they learned that day. If they didn’t come prepared to share something, they would have to leave until they found something to learn about.

One day, Patrik (12) told us he learned about worms that could live inside of a dog. Kevin commented that he had probably picked up some parasites while in Korea as a missionary. Patrik was quick to quip, "That's because you ate dog soup!"

What good luck is...

Morfar, Dad, Brayden and an Uncle went golfing and came home to tell a bit about their round. Apparently Daddy came close to getting a hole in one. Sean (7) said he had done a good job and then quickly reversed his opinion without explanation. Of course we were all curious as to why he did this. Sean seemed to think it all very logical. "Because," he said in a matter of fact tone, "otherwise you would have had to buy the rest of these guys a beer afterwards."

The upside and the downside.

A friend had a baby shower for me and I got to take some balloons home from it. The day after the shower, obviously the balloons no longer had helium holding them up. Derek (5) decided to play with one and was excited to find that "it has a little Helaman!" (a person from the Book of Mormon)

Then as it sank to the ground he sadly proclaimed, "It has a little gravity too."

About migration...

In a contemplative mood, Sean (9) stared out the window at some birds. "Mom", Sean asked, "Which way is south?"

I pointed in a general southern direction.

Then, in an "Aha! Gotcha!" tone of voice, Sean said, "Then why are those birds flying north??!!"

Hand-me-downs are great.

Malena (2 ½) was looking at her dresses in the closet. She pointed to one and said, "I really like this one." I told her that the little orange summer dress was one that her cousin's Mom gave to her.

She looked back up at me with a quizzical expression on her face and questioned, "It was too teeny for his Mom?"

One thing leads to another.

Intelligent, logical conversation--Brayden (14) was sculpting a bust of a guy with a ponytail. Malena (4) came in the room and asked, "Who is that?"

Brayden answered that he wasn't sure.

"Well," says Malena, "It looks like George Washington." (Brayden was making a colonial looking figure)

Brayden was surprised she knew about Washington. Malena then wondered where he lived. We explained that he is dead now, so he lives in heaven. Being more insistent, she wanted to know where he lives! We told her about Mt. Vernon. I guess she decided our answers weren't good enough. "I wish I could talk to him," she said. "But, I don't know his phone number."

We then explained that he wouldn't have even known about phones. She, of course, had a ready answer for that. We would have to make a cool phone for him. But, it would have to be Patrik (16) that made the phone. "Why Patrik?" asked Brayden.

"Because he can make cool planes" was the reason she gave.

Ah, but of course…

Yesterday I went into the bathroom and on the counter was our hand soap dispenser which was tied to a folding chair with a cloth belt. The culprit was Malena (5). When asked why she did this, she said, "So the chair wouldn't move."

There's always a reason.

Malena (5 ½) just came in here with a pouty face. I asked her what was going on. She says, "Patrik (17) told me he won't read me a story because I spanked his butt for no reason." Here there is a short pause, and then she continues as the tears start to come, "But, I did have a reason!" Sob, sob.

The reason? "He said he would only read me one story instead of two!"

It ain't over 'til it's over.

The boys were all paying attention to the ball game and their team had just blown a big lead late in the game. Kevin commented that it was all over. One of the boys corrected him by saying it was just the 8th inning. "Yeah," Sean (13) quipped, "but the fat lady is warming up."

You get your best logical thinking by focusing on facts. Bet you didn't know this.

Patrik (4 ½) let us know that when it rains, turtles turn into seashells.

Church terminology:

Patrik (5) thinks Kevin teaches the "dinkins" at church (instead of Deacons).

Nursing babies get good stuff.

Patrik (5) thinks that when Sean nurses he drinks milk from one side and honey from the other. I'm not sure where he got that from.

How good is that?

Manda (3 ½) told Daddy today there was "frosting" on the grass.

You can learn a lot from Disney.

Pointing to my round stomach, I asked Sean (2), "What's this?"

He told me "Pooh tummick!"

I said, "What's in it?"

He told me matter-of-factly, "Honey."

Save money by telling others what is going on in your life.

My daughter (7), the monkey, climbed up our back wall yesterday and scooted across a whole length of it. She has also just about made it to the top of the pine tree, which she decided to try out. She has been climbing on these other things because her favorite climbing tree attracted a large horde of bees, which were there for about 1 ½ to 2 weeks.

I called a beekeeper to come and get them; but the night they came, the bees were gone and so was our $35 for a service call even though no work was done. The next morning we told the kids the bees were gone and Amanda said, "I know, they have been gone for a couple of days."

Too bad she didn't tell us that and we could have paid her $10 instead of shelling out $35 to the bee guy! Oh well!

What make-up really does for a person.

Brayden (6) was studying me as I was putting on my mascara. "Why do you do that?" he asked.

I told him the reason was to make my lashes look thicker and longer. This caused him to get a rather strange look on his face. I asked him if something was wrong with that, and did he not like the way it looked.

He said, "Not really. It makes your eyes look like seeds, or like owl's eyes or something."

The right definition is...

Sean (5) asked me if I knew what an expert was. I told him it was someone who was really good at something or knew a lot about something.

"Nope, that's not it." He said back to me.

So I asked him what an expert is.

"Well, it's kind of like what you said, but they can do it with their eyes closed."

And, here's what guns do.

It is an election year this year and we were at the table discussing some political topics. The subject of gun control was brought up and one of the kids asked what that meant. I facetiously said, "It is when the government won't let anybody own a gun because guns kill people."
Sean, the five year-old, cuts me off at this point by saying, "No, they do not!"

I said, "Oh really?"

Sean very knowingly responded, "Guns don't kill people, the bad guys do."

If a five-year-old can understand that concept, why can't grown-ups? Then we talked about how the club that Cain used to slay Abel wasn't responsible for the act, and etc.

Get your words straight.

I said something about the candy "smarties" making a person stupid or something like that. Derek (8) was quick to comment that it wasn't smarties responsible for that, "you get stupid from eating dum-dums!" he said.

Quit when it is time to quit.

> Sitting at the dinner table today, Kevin told us a stupid joke about pirates. Then he decided to keep speaking in "piratese". It was becoming obnoxious, so I borrowed part of a familiar phrase by saying, "the horse is dead, Kev."
>
> Brayden (14) made my words all the more effective by adding his own, "Yep, but the chariot's still rolling."

Trouble is that children tend to take everything you say very literally. You have to make sure that your directions are always clear!

Be obedient.

> The kids were sorting a couple cases of peaches for me (taking out the bad ones). I picked up one with some growth on it and told them if they have this fuzzy stuff on it, put it in this box, if they look all right, they go in the other box. Well a few minutes later I checked on their progress. The box of yucky ones had grown substantially and as I watched I could see that Manda (7) would carefully select a peach, quickly look at it and put every one she picked into the yucky box.
>
> I said, "Manda, why are you putting them all in the yucky box?"

She said, "All these ones are fuzzy!"

I guess I used a bad term to describe how to find the yucky peaches when I said fuzzy, huh? She certainly was following orders well.

It's always good to follow directions precisely…or not.

I sent Brayden, Derek and Sean to the tub this afternoon. After a few minutes I went to check up on them. Brayden was busy lathering up his hair with shampoo. The only trouble is that he put the shampoo on, but no water. I asked him why he hadn't wet his hair down first. He said, "But Mom, this is shampoo for dry hair."

I started snickering and couldn't stop. He continued to explain, "See, it says it right here on the bottle. Shampoo for dry hair." Heh. Heh. Heh. (It still makes me snicker!)

It is easy to win when you put your mind to it.

I asked Malena (3) and Derek (8) to clean up what they were playing with. Malena had dominoes that came in a box where you have to stack the dominoes about 8 across, 6 wide, and 4 deep. Derek had Jenga blocks which are stored in a tall narrow container. I told Malena to see if she could beat Derek by filling hers up to the top first. Very soon I heard I little voice exclaim, "I beat him! Mine is full up to the top!"

Not thinking it was possible for her to be done that quickly; I had to have a look. She did indeed have it full up to the top. The only problem was that it was a single stack. There were still about 30 or more dominoes on the floor! But, she did what I asked.

~ Chapter 13

Positive Thinking

I think children have positive thinking automatically wired into their systems. They always have answers.

Yup, that'll work.

> Daddy didn't have enough money, so Patrik (3) told him he had to get some. "Where am I going to get some?" Daddy asked.
>
> Patrik knew the answer, "You need to buy some!"

Getting it right...

> Patrik (3) and I went to watch Daddy's ball game. When the opponent hurried to cross home plate, Patrik applauded him while loudly cheering "Yes! Yes!" Then he said to me, "Look Mom, he ran a good one. He went to home!"
>
> I said to Patrik, "Yes, he did run well, but unfortunately he is on the wrong team."

This did not discourage Patrik. He then said, "Oh. Maybe next time he'll get on the right team."

That sounds great!

I asked Daddy if he wanted to grill fish on Saturday. Patrik (4) piped up saying, "Yeah, and I want a boy fish".

Too true...

Yesterday Kevin was playing catch with Brayden (2 ½). He tossed Brayden the ball which bounced off his chest, rolled down his arms and then across the floor. Brayden quickly ran over and picked up the ball, which he then handed to me. He then informed me that, "That was a bad throw, Dad".

Dad said, "No, it wasn't—that was a bad catch."

He retorted, "No, Dad. I didn't catch it!"

Living with "Murphy" sure gives life its ups and downs.

Murphy's Law seems to prevail too much around here. Yesterday, I put a large pot full of honey on the stove because it had hardened and I needed it to liquefy again. I turned it on and then I left to go help Sean (3) clean his room.

By the time I got done with that and handling a couple of minor issues, I went back to the kitchen to find that half of the honey was gone from the pot. It was such a mess. It boiled over so it was a half-inch thick of goo under the burners and my stovetop doesn't lift up!

Later on, I let Patrik (8) help me make a fruit drink in the blender. When there was liquid in the blender, he scooped another scoop of peaches with a huge plop into the blender and 'splat' it all sprayed out on Mom's head and I had just washed my hair!

Always there's something.

More Murphy...

The bad news is "CRASH!" I hear Amanda (7) drop a full glass (yes, glass-glass) of juice.

The good news is the cup miraculously did not break.

The bad news is there is juice splattered all over the linoleum.

The good news is it didn't get on the carpet.

The bad news is she wants more so she steals mine.

The good news is there was still enough to go around.

The bad news is Patrik (8) steps in the puddle and continues walking.

So, I wonder, did I come out even?

The finer things in life make life better.

This morning I didn't feel like grinding up wheat for flour and making up pancakes from scratch, so I made some from Bisquick mix. When I put the plate of freshly made pancakes on the table Amanda (8) exclaimed, "Ooooh! Pancakes like at Grandma's house."

Brayden (7) chimed in with, "Yeah, now all we need is bacon, eggs, and Grandpa!"

This is the way it is and the way it is going to be, period!

Yesterday when Malena (2) woke up she had a big mosquito bite on her cheek. So, I explained what it was.

She said, "No, I bonked onna door."

I said, "No, a bug bit you."

She responded, "No, a ball hit me on my cheek!"

I tried once more, to which she emphatically replied, "No, a bug not eat me all gone!"

If you know what you want, it is easier to think in a positive direction. I have learned that you really need to make up your mind.

Amanda (3) had a rough night. She got in bed with Mom and Dad. "I'm hungry," she said.

We asked her what she wanted to eat. She said, "ummm" a few times and then was quiet.

About 5 or 10 minutes later as Mom and Dad were falling back asleep, we heard a little voice say, "... ummm, pancakes!"

We laughed. Then, as sleep was about to overtake us, amid sounds of "ummm" every so often, we heard the little voice again. This time it said, "...ummm, sandwich."

If at first you don't succeed...

Brayden (2 ½) was playing with a little plastic duck. He seemed like he was getting a bit frustrated with the duck because he kept banging it on the counter. While banging, he would say, "Come out!" and keep repeating the command, "Come out!" over and over.

I figured out what the problem was when he finally said, "That egg won't come out!"

If you want to get somewhere, keep at it. It'll happen.

> Sean (5 ½ months) has started to crawl, but does more scooting than crawling just yet. He gets on his hands and knees, but then he gets up on his feet and hands and digs his toes in the carpet to push himself forward. Sean loves to stand and walk. In fact, it is sometimes difficult to get him to sit. He tries desperately to avoid sitting by keeping his body stiff as a board if you try to set him down. You can put him down to where his head is an inch from the ground and he still won't bend. He also loves to get shoulder and horsey rides from sister and brothers (with a little balancing help from Mom).

Make a living doing something you enjoy.

> I told Sean (2) he needed to help make his bed and put away his books. "Why?" he wanted to know.
>
> I informed him, "Because it is your job."
>
> He was not too happy about that. Shortly thereafter he came marching determinedly out of his bedroom, golf clubs in tow. "This is my job!" he said, pointing to the clubs.

Big kids do more.

> Sean (3) is learning so many new things. He writes and traces things and does matching games when the other kids do their school papers. He is getting better at cleaning up. I just tell him if he doesn't help, then the big kids will think he is a little kid and won't let him play Legos with him next time, just like they don't let Derek play. Then after thinking a bit he jumps up and says, "I'm a big boy, actually." (sounds like ak-shoo-uh-ly)

Sneaky tactics work.

> I was in the bathroom curling my hair and I heard a scratching sound on the door. Then I heard, "Mamaaaa!" More scratching towards the bottom of the door. I looked down. There was one of Derek's (1) favorite storybooks, which he had slid under the door to give me a hint that it was time to read him a story. Of course I couldn't resist that ploy.

You can get a good deal of mileage by engaging the help of an assistant.

> Sean (4) has found a new avenue to pursue in trying to get what he wants. He enlists the help of his 18-month-old brother. It goes something like this, with Sean saying, "Tanny, (His nickname for Derek) do you want to watch a video?"

Then he coaches him, "Say YEAH! YEAH! YEAH!"

Then Derek gets excited about it and joins in the chant, saying, "YEAH! YEAH! YEAH!" Then Mom has to think twice before saying no to both of them!

The ultimate occupation is...

The kids are now in school at an academy, which meets 3 days a week from 8 until noon. I teach the beginning class, which consists of 12 four to six year old children. One of the things we do in class is story time during which I read a story to the kids.

I was reading a story called "Maybe you should fly a jet, maybe you should be a vet." The book goes through listing several occupations a child might want to have when he grows up. I let the children holler out "Yes!" or "No!" according to whether they would like to have that job or not.

I read the suggestions, including fireman, ballet dancer, rollercoaster owner, baker, circus clown and many others. I didn't hear a peep out of Sean (4 ½) the whole time. He must have been considering his options deeply. Finally I read money loaner. Then immediately I hear Sean's excited voice yell, "Yes! I want to be a money owner!"

Yo-yo-ing can be fun.

Malena (1 ½) also likes to go to the front window and scream, "Wibby" (meaning Liberty the neighbor's dog). But then if Libby shows up in our yard, she hollers equally exuberantly, "Shoooo!"

If you get all dressed up, ya gotta go somewhere!

Malena (1 ½) loves to be outside. She will question, "Ou?"

Then if you don't respond favorably, she will say, "shoos?" and "ha?".

If that doesn't get results, she will go find a pair of shoes and a hat, regardless of whether they belong to her and plead again, "Ou?"

How do you resist that??

Two year olds can give some very good descriptions.

Today Malena (2) came to me and had to try really hard to put into words what she wanted to convey. She pointed to her bug bite and said, "I need, I need...I need this not to be hot."

The bite is fairly large and somewhat swollen from scratching it, so I am sure it is hot!

Know how to work the system.

> Malena (6) was at her friend's house last night and was supposed to stay for a couple of hours. After a couple of hours, the friend's Mom called to see if we minded that she let the girls watch a movie before bringing Malena home. She told me that Malena had given her very specific instructions on how to ask her parents if she could stay longer. "If the first parent says no, then you have to ask the other parent."

~ Chapter 14

Choose the Right

Try to fix your mistakes before you get into too much trouble.

> I went into the bedroom to check what Brayden (1) was doing. As I walked in I saw that he had taken half of Daddy's pants out of the drawer. I only had a chance to say, "Oh, Brayden." before Brayden decided to hurriedly finish my sentence. He was shaking his finger at me, saying "no-no" over and over. Then he started shoveling everything back in the drawer!

Sometimes the kids come through for you very well.

> A couple days ago, I had a huge mound of clothes on the couch to fold. I sat down and got busy. Patrik (6) looked at me and said, "Mom, do you want me to help you fold those?"
>
> I said, "Sure."

He started pitching in and then said in a very grown-up manner, "I saw that there was a lot of clothes, so I thought you could use some help, because it goes faster with two helping."

Isn't that sweet?

Speaking nicely will get you stuff.

I was enjoying a bowl of oatmeal. Sean (almost 2) came, wanting some. I got some for him, which he finished, before I could finish mine. He then started being whiny and grumpy and crabby and pointing at my food. I said, "Sean, can you talk a little more nicely."

He was quiet for just a second before he stuck his little round face between two chubby hands, looked at me with big blue eyes, and said earnestly, "Peaz, Mom?"

Needless to say, he ate most of the rest of my food.

Pray before every meal.

Sean (3) was the only one up and ready for breakfast. I gave him some food and he asked if I would please bless it. I did so. Sean complimented me saying, "That was a lovely prayer."

Make sure everyone is happy.

Brayden (1 ½) found a quarter, showed it to me, and said, "Money". I asked, "Is that Morfar's money?"

"No," said Brayden.

Then he thought for a moment, picked up the remote control for the television, looked at me and said, "Share?" He ran over and gave Morfar the remote and kept the quarter for himself.

When you share, it helps others.

Brayden (13) couldn't find the answer key to his math the other day and asked me what to do about it. "I don't have an answer key for this lesson", he said.

Malena (3) comes running up happily to provide the solution to his problem, "I have an answer key! You can use it!" (She is holding a key that opens doors.)

Sharing solves many problems.

There was a lizard in my room!!! I thought it was fake at first until it moved. I screamed!

Patrik (14) and Brayden (12) came and tore apart my room looking for it. It was not found. Kev was at a ball game with Sean. I called him to complain & fuss. He told me I'd be fine. I said I wouldn't, seeing as how lizards can climb bedposts and everything.

Derek (6) comforted me later by letting me know I could sleep in his room. "I don't have any bedposts in my room!"

Always cheer up the sad and make someone feel glad.

Mommy was having a bad day and started crying. Patrik (3) looked at me and said "Mom, you have mud on you face!" (Mascara)

Comfort the sick.

We were eating dinner out at Skippers and when the guy in the booth across the aisle sneezed, Brayden said, "Bless you."

Incredulous, the guy turned and looked at Brayden. "What did you say?" he asked our little 1-year-old.

Kevin said, "He told you bless you. Say it again Brayden."

Brayden said it many more times. I do believe the man became convinced that his ears had not deceived him.

Remember the poor.

We took Daddy some lunch at a construction site where he was washing windows. I looked around and said, "Where do you go if you have to go potty?"

Daddy said, "See that portable John over there?"

After a few moments of thought, Patrik (4) asked us, "What's the matter with 'Poor old John?"

Give good advice.

Mom and Dad were leaving on a date and as we were heading out the door, Amanda (4) rushed up to me. She looked me deeply in the eyes, paused, and very seriously said, "Be sure to be careful so you don't crash."

Mourn with those that mourn.

Brayden (3) came to me and said, "Mommy, I need to tell you something".

I asked him what it was. He thought for a moment before looking back at me with wide blue eyes and saying, "When we die, our bones have to stay here all alone."

He was feeling very sad for our bones. He brightened up after I told him about the resurrection again.

Repent of wrong doing.

> Sean (2) is saying a lot now. He is very polite; he always says 'Thank you' and 'excuse me'. The only time I can get him to say 'sorry', though, is when someone else is the one who is supposed to say it!

Think of those that are less fortunate than yourself.

> Sean (2 ½) just said to me, "Mom, you have to make Derek (5 months) some teeth!"

Help those in need of help.

> Patrik (8) spent the better part of the day a few days ago helping mom clean, fold laundry, etc. He wanted to be helping mom instead of out playing with the kids. It is really sweet of him how he likes to help out.

Save the world.

> Patrik (8) has been reading a few books about endangered species. He came and told me he would like to read more about them because it makes him sad to think that some of them are going to be extinct. He said he would like to read more to see what he can do to help them when he is a grown up.

I thought that was quite thoughtful of him, but I don't really want him running off to join the EPA or anything. So, I asked him for his opinion of the following scenario. If a man owned several acres of land and he wanted to build a building on his property, but there were endangered species on his land, should the government tell him he couldn't build?

Patrik thought just for a minute to digest the info, and then replied, "No, because that would be bossy."

Then he said, "They (the government) don't do that today, do they?" (Inferring that they used to, perhaps, but in today's society they wouldn't because we know better.)

Anyway, after learning that these things do indeed happen, Patrik thought the simple solution would be to just fire those corrupt people in our government.

We also talked about some ideas of what could be done better. Patrik suggested making a building to give to the people who are studying them.

Solve the problem of the homeless.

We have a jar with slips of paper that have questions on them that is supposed to be used

to help stimulate good table conversations. A question posed to Sean (3 ½) was this:
"What do you think of when you see a homeless person?"

Sean had a perfect answer. "I think he should go live with someone else."

Make others feel good about themselves.

Mormor and Morfar were enjoying Sean's (5) birthday cake with us. Brayden (8) offered Mormor a second slice of cake. She declined by saying that she better not since she was too fat.

Brayden, who is the diplomatic one, charmed her by saying, "Oh Mormor, you are not fat."

Mormor was momentarily happy that her sweet grandson thought to tell her that until she heard the rest of his comment. He continued, "Chubby, yes, but not fat."

Here's the truth, the whole truth and nothing but the truth!

Lena (3) loves salad. When she had finished her second helping of salad very quickly, I teasingly said, "Daddy, what happened to Lena's salad?"

He joined in the teasing as he looked at her and said, "Did you throw your salad on the floor?"

"No," she promptly replied, "just my 'mato."

And yes, there was her tomato on the floor. When Kevin picked it up, she grabbed it and popped it into her mouth.

Never tell a lie!

We've had relatives in town for Patrik's (18) graduation. With Grandpa staying at our house, I threw my bathrobe on over my pajamas. I don't wear my bathrobe often because it is rather hot. So, when we all gathered for family prayer, Malena (6) asked, "Why do you have that on?"

Rather than go into any long explanations I just said, "I am trying to maintain some sense of modesty."

She chuckled and came right back with, "No, Mom, tell me the truth!"

Make sure to keep your priorities in life straight.

Malena (4) has a friend over today. I just overheard this conversation.

Malena: I wish it was church day today.
Friend: Why?
Malena: Because then we could do singing. I love singing.

Friend: Yeah, me too. Singing is my life.
Malena: Yeah, it's my life too.
Friend: And, candy is my second life.

You never know what kids will come up with that they are thankful for. They will often think of things that I wouldn't have.

Being sandwiched between two boys, Amanda sometimes got lost in the shuffle. She was pretty thankful that she had something all her own. Not hand-me-down boy clothes, no focusing on the brothers, just something for Manda…

Amanda celebrated her 2 year old birthday today. She received lots of presents. She got a baby doll that came with a tiny potty-chair and a tiny bottle. She got some cute outfits as well. Bambi shorts outfit and denim shorts overalls with pink trim were two articles of clothing she got. She got teddy bear books and Disney read along books too. Each present she opened we asked her what it was. "Mine!" she would say in response.

Sometimes it is just awesome being around the people you love most.

On a very busy Sunday, Daddy had several meetings to attend. In between meetings, he came home to spend a little time with his family. After kissing the kids good-bye for my next trip to the church, Brayden (2 ½) looked up at Kevin and said, "Thank you for coming, Dad."

One should always take pleasure in unexpected surprises!

We were making cookies and Mom wound up burning a couple of trays of cookies. Amanda (4 ½), who loves burnt toast, burnt parts of lasagna, etc., asked me "Mommy, did you burn these just for me?"

Living and breathing is no small thing.

Patrik (8) fell off a rocky cliff and fractured his cheekbone. Like he said to me when he first saw me, "I am just glad I am alive."

My sentiments exactly. His face was swollen up about 20 times its normal size.

We should always be clean; morally and physically.

Brayden (2) was eating some cereal and had only milk left in the bowl. He put both hands in the milk and wiggled his fingers around. I said, "Oh Brayden, don't play in the milk".

Brayden just told me very matter-of-factly, "I have to wash my hands!"

Working is a very important part of choosing the right. Believe it or not, kids really enjoy working at a young age. Perhaps it is that when they get older they discover that it is no fun. It is awesome while it lasts though.

Patrik, Amanda and Brayden (at 4, 3, and 2) can wash and stack most all the dishes into the dishwasher. Brayden gets completely drenched and often puts things in the dishwasher wrong, but he sure enjoys it. He even gets mad when we run out of dishes to wash!

Work is easier and more fun when everyone pitches in.

I have started a new thing with the kids that's working well. Each day I have 3 helper jobs: kitchen, vacuum, and laundry. They rotate turns 6 days of the week and on the 7th is "on request" day. Today for instance, any cooking or cleaning I do in the kitchen, Brayden (3) is on call to help with that. Amanda (4) helps out with the vacuuming and Patrik (5) is on laundry duty. They all have been very good about it and very happy to have their turn, especially if it is kitchen duty! (2008 note: Boy do times change! I still try out new things to try to get them to clean up, but rarely is anyone happy about any cleaning duty! Am I doing something wrong? Or does everyone grow up with an aversion to cleaning?)

Some things are worth getting up for.

We just got ourselves a Manx cat (tail-less) from the relief society president. Amanda is the kitty's new mom. The first morning after we had her, she was meowing at about 7:00 a.m. Amanda jumped right out of bed the second she heard the kitty and went out to 'check on her'. It was quite funny because Amanda was still only half awake as she came scurrying down the hall. I don't even know how she could hear that tiny mew from her room.

It's a hard life, but somebody's gotta do it!

A couple days ago, Patrik (13) went with his Dad to work. Actually, Patrik went to play while Dad worked. He hit a lot of golf balls and worked on some scout stuff while he was there. After they got home, Patrik quickly changed and they headed off to his baseball game. They grabbed a bite to eat on the way home and then Patrik had a birthday party to attend for one of his buddies.

The following morning Patrik had a tough time getting out of bed. Dad told him to stop his complaining. He grumpily retorted, "Why don't you see how you feel after playing golf and baseball all day and then going to a party 'til late!"

Both Kevin and I were quick with our eager responses, "Ooh! Pick me!"

(Later when he was more fully awake, he did seem to acknowledge, sheepishly, that it was a foolish statement.)

~ Chapter 15

Be Happy with Who You Are

When you are happy to be you, it is easier to love others. Children love everyone, including themselves.

Entertain yourself.

> Amanda's (4 ½) humor is very different than the boys. She always comes up with really unexpected funnies. For instance, Kevin and I were getting kids shoes on to go somewhere and we heard the front door slowly creaking open. We look over and see no one, until Manda's little head peeks around the corner.
>
> She looked at us and said, "Boo!" Then she retreated quickly while quietly giggling to herself.

We can be all friends.

> When Aunt M first moved to live near us, Sean pointed at his cousin and said in a fascinated tone of voice, "He same old like me!" They got along quite nicely with the hot wheels.

Some things are just really the pits!

> Derek (4) was twisting his lips as far as he could to one side of his face. He kept trying again and again. Finally, dejected, he gave up and said, "I can not kiss my cheek."

Life is good!

> Malena (4 months) is a very cheerful baby. She smiles easily and frequently. She is right now at a stage of rolling around and around and around! The other day I had her on a blanket in the front room and she rolled to one corner of the blanket. Then she grabbed hold of that corner and rolled back so she wrapped herself up like a cocoon. All that was showing was her cute little face and boy was she proud of herself!

> Malena is also trying to grab for anything that comes anywhere close to her. One time as I was bending over to get something out of the fridge she reached out and grabbed Patrik by the ear. Patrik leaped in surprise. He was busy doing his schoolwork at the desk and wasn't anticipating any such attack!

It is wonderful to be able to explore.

> Malena (7 months) got her first tooth today. She won't, of course, let us see it. You can

feel the little razor sharp thing though on her bottom gum. She is crawling around quite handily now. She has discovered the bookcase, electrical cords, and other no-nos. She seldom puts scraps of paper and other small items she finds on the floor in her mouth, which is a great blessing since there are frequently such items on the floor. She growls and babbles, blows bubbles and giggles, but she still is not too interested in solid food.

Sample some of everything. You might like it!

Yay! Malena (8 months) has discovered that eating cheerios is fun. She also has decided that one other food is delicious. It is cooked celery bits. We had homemade chicken noodle soup the other day and she absolutely loved the celery in that. She has decided now that all tiny objects should be put into the mouth. You know, like rocks, paper scraps, old dried up pea someone missed when sweeping, and other lovely items. She waves bye-bye frequently now too.

Babies learn an incredible amount in short amounts of time.

Malena (9 months) now can stand without anything to help herself up. She will just stand there in the middle of the room for a while until she notices that she isn't holding on to anything. Then she quickly sits down. She always crawls on hands and feet (not knees) She can wave bye-bye, signal come here with her hand, throw something when you tell her to, and hide things behind her back that she thinks you might want to take from her. She still jabbers a whole bunch. She loves the pool. She cries if Amanda leaves the room without taking her with her. (I think Amanda has gained a shadow for life.) She likes ice and pretzels best for food right now. You can see some of the 5 teeth that are now protruding if you look closely. She loves to be outside, especially enjoying the trampoline.

Disguise yourself well.

We went to a fall carnival. They had rock climbing, one of those jumping things, fish and get a prize, and other games. They also did movie popcorn, homemade root beer, cotton candy, hot dogs & chili. I had asked the kids if they wanted to wear a costume. They all said they didn't want to.

Then Sean (8) changed his mind. "Actually, I will go as Derek." I thought that was perfect, since those two are constantly mistaken. So, Patrik and Brayden dressed alike and went as each other and Sean and Derek did that too. Manda, Malena, and I all wore Pooh Bear overalls. Kevin was a golf pro—original, huh?

Always try to be of good service to others.

We had a garage sale, at which Malena (1) was very helpful. She would wander around looking at all the toys and peel off various price stickers and place them on herself.

You are who you are, and there's nothing you can do about it.

Looking at a picture of a bunch of the cousins, Lena (2 ½) was dismayed when Daddy pointed out Lena in the picture. It was a picture taken of her when she was less than a year old and she didn't have much hair. At first, she would not accept that it was herself. After a while, she decided that if it had to be her she felt she had to justify it by saying, "I was a boy."

Believe you are royalty.

We often call Malena (3) a princess. A couple days ago she went up and asked her Daddy, "When do I get locked up in a castle?"

When Kevin laughed, she explained, "That's what the bad guys do with princesses. Then the good guys save her."

Stand up for those too small to do it themselves.

> A certain Uncle likes to call Brayden (8 months) "Buddy", and whenever he does this, Amanda (1 ½) is quick to correct him "No Buddy! Baby!"

Have a blast!

> Malena (1 ½) likes to go on the little tikes slide. She climbs up and says, "up, up, up".
>
> Then as she slides down she gleefully squeals, "wheeeeee!"

If you are happy in your own skin, you won't be afraid to use your talents.

Learn to surprise people now and then.

> Amanda (14) had an awards/concert for her school that was definitely worth going to. Manda had a solo song that she did. I knew that. What I didn't know is what song she was performing or what she was doing with it. She sang "Only in America". I was very startled because when the music started, my daughter all of a sudden started jammin' out with a fake guitar. It was hilarious but awesome. She did a great job. She has no fear in front of people when it comes to singing. There were probably 200+ people there.

I should be more easily entertained.

> Brayden (6) came to me and said, "Hey, mom! Do you want to see what I can do with my

nose?" I turned to look. He pulled out the harmonica and played a lovely melody on it through his nose!

Little children have the best ability to be happy for others. This is evident when someone's birthday rolls around. The youngest in our family always joins in to help the birthday boy or girl unwrap presents. The little one is always excited to see what there is, even though the gift isn't theirs.

You should always be excited to see those you love succeed at difficult tasks.

So, Wynter (3 ½ months) rolled over yesterday. Malena (5) was there and saw him do it. She took off like a flash of lightning. Shortly thereafter, I heard the thundering of many feet running down the hallway. She had broadcasted the word to her brothers in the other room who had to come charging in to see the momentous occasion.

Wynter rolled over again and they exploded in applause and shouts of, "Way to go Wynter!" The poor baby lay there looking a little stunned at his enthusiastic audience.

Be free with compliments.

I haphazardly tossed a couple of potholders onto the table, one right after the other. Both landed in the same spot. Patrik (15) commented, "Nice shot, Mom."

I said, "And how did you like my form?"

He came up with this description, "It was fresh and new."

Or, just say it how you see it.

I crawled over to Derek (3) and asked him, "Do you know what I need?"

He gave me a grin and replied, "A kiss."

After I received my kiss, I said, "Derek, you have the sweetest face."

He looked at me with those big eyes and says, "Yeah, and you have...a nose. With these on (points to my glasses)."

I asked him, "Where did we get you from?"

He unhesitatingly responded, "In Africa."

~ Chapter 16

Get a Grip, Mom & Dad!

Do you ever do dumb things? One of my sons told me the other day that we could probably write a book just on all the silly things Mom has done. Too bad I never wrote all those things down. Then again, maybe not!

> Sometimes mothers can be so embarrassing. I took Patrik (11) and Brayden (9) up to baseball tryouts and then had to run Amanda (10) somewhere else. I had left them with a bunch of fruit and other munchies to keep their energy up. I also was sure to leave them with plenty of water because it was quite warm out. I was a little worried because I know that Patrik in particular is very susceptible to heat stroke when he hasn't had enough liquid. So when I came back, I noticed, thankfully, that Patrik's water bottle was almost empty.
>
> Brayden's, on the other hand, was nearly full. I was rather concerned. So, I went down by the baseball field where Brayden was playing around with some of the other kids awaiting their turns for tryouts. I called Brayden over

and told him he needed to have some more water. While he was obediently drinking I reminded him how important it is to drink a lot of water in the heat. He finished swallowing, looked me in the eye and said, "Mom, I have already filled this up three times at the water fountain!"

Is it just a lack of sleep issue? Or something deeper?

Mother has been having problems lately with switching words around and inputting incorrect words, but you can just imagine the look on Derek's (5) face when I told him to throw some scraps in the trash and jump in the garbage. (He actually needed to go get a bath.)

Mother!

A few days ago, I was sitting on the couch and Brayden (9) came over to me with a bottle of lotion. He plopped down on the floor and started massaging my feet and my calves. (This isn't too unusual; he often gives me unexpected massages). As he was working on my left foot, I had an amusing thought and I giggled a little bit. Brayden asked me if the massage tickled.

I said "No, actually, I was just thinking about how much your future wife is going to appreciate you."

The look on his face was priceless. His face flamed in three shades of red and his eyes rolled up in one of the most embarrassed looks I have ever seen. If he had said something, I am sure it would have been one of those sing-song exasperated "Mom!" things that kids say when embarrassed by their mother.

Sometimes I go overboard with my worries.

Kevin called me last night at about 9:30 when he arrived at Boy Scout camp. Here's what he told me. "Brayden (12) is pretty beat up. He was in a bike accident a couple days ago. He has blood all over his face, a fat lip, two chipped teeth and a hurt knee."

One of my first questions was why he has blood all over his face if this happened a couple of days ago. The response? "This is scout camp. You don't shower up here." (AARGH)

(Here the reader better take a deep breath.) So then the guilt sets in—oh no! I should have packed some BFC (herbal salve that heals everything 10 times faster) into his first aid kit! I wish I could be there and clean him up and cry with him! Yada yada yada. AND, today is his birthday. I was supposed to go pick him up and bring him back here so he could try out for all-stars for baseball, so I didn't send any presents up with Kevin for him. And now, he is not in good enough shape to tryout, so he is just staying at camp until tomorrow and coming home with everyone else. This is his first weeklong scout campout.

I talked to him on the phone last night. He was doing all right until he talked to me and that made him cry. So then when I hung up the phone I cried. I told the little boys Brayden wasn't coming till Saturday. They were upset. Sean cried and moped for about 45 minutes. Waaaaah! (Okay, you can breathe again now)

Sometimes your own logic can be used against you.

Malena (4) has a house that Brayden (14) made for her from a cardboard box. Kevin accidently spilled a cup full of water that splashed all over her house. As he was cleaning it up, he was trying to convince her in a rather repetitive manner that everything was alright by telling her that she should pretend it had rained. Malena wasn't buying that idea. But, Kevin persisted, "Where's your imagination? You have to use your imagination and just pretend it is rain."

Malena let him know that she had her imagination in her head, but she was not going to give in to the rain idea. It just didn't seem right to her.

About an hour later, Malena asked if we could have dessert. I said we could have dessert tomorrow. Kevin confirmed my plan by saying that we would eat dessert after Sunday dinner tomorrow. It didn't take long for Malena to say this to her Daddy, "Can't we just pretend it is tomorrow?"

The mean ol' grouch.

I asked Malena (5) the other day why she and her best friend seemed to be spending way more time at her friend's house than ours lately. I asked her if it was because I am such a mean ol' grouch.

She chuckled and said, "No, you aren't... but Dad is."

I told her he certainly isn't always grouchy and to demonstrate, I reminded her of when he tucks her in at night, plays games with her, and reads her stories. She said, "Yes, but sometimes he gets mad <u>even</u> at me!"

~ Chapter 17

Miscellaneous Tidbits

Here I give you a final random category to toss in all those lovely bits of wisdom that didn't seem to fit elsewhere.

Sometimes, things just go wrong, no matter what you do. And I thought I had it bad...

> Sean (3 ½) asked for more and more seasoning on his rice, saying, "I can't taste any!"
>
> I said there must be something wrong with his taste buds.
>
> "Yeah," he said forlornly, "they melted."

Ooh! Hate it when that happens.

> We have a jar with slips of paper that have questions on them that is supposed to be used to help stimulate good table conversations. A question posed to Sean (3 ½) was this: "Have you ever felt out of place?"
>
> Sean answered seriously "Yes, I did!"

> Then the next question asks "When?"
>
> Sean immediately answered, "In my bed!"

There are times when you just don't feel like getting up.

> This morning, after several failed attempts at awakening Derek (9), we decided to try a new trick. We put my cell phone on the pillow beside him. Then, Kevin called my phone repeatedly.
>
> No response.
>
> Finally, Kevin went to Derek and asked, "Didn't you hear the phone?"
>
> "Yes," came the disgruntled reply, "And it was getting annoying!"

Things should be the way God intended them to be.

> Sean (10) is, and always has been, appalled to the point of being horrified at immodesty in females. For instance, a commercial came on TV the other day with a dancing woman who was Marilyn Monroe-esque in her dress. Sean shrieked a prolonged "EEEEWWW" and made us change the station immediately.
>
> Today, he has a history lesson in which the first question is a role playing situation and

asks, "You are a woman in England...what do you do then?" Sean says emphatically, "Now that is just wrong!"

Why does the good stuff always disappear so quickly??

We were sitting at the table for dinner where Derek (3) had been enjoying his chicken. He turned around to say something to someone behind him. When he turned back around he looked at his plate and his little face became very dismayed. With his lower lip jutting out and sad blue eyes, he stared at the puddle of gravy that was left on his plate and declared, "My chicken melted!"

Here are a few items all having to do with some cartoon or another...

Don't be afraid to have some imaginary fun.

One day at dinner time, Kevin decided to have a little fun with the kids. Somehow he decided to start an imaginary "food fight" with the kids like they do in Disney's "Hook". He threw an imaginary piece of food at Patrik (9). Patrik responded by throwing his own food at Kevin. Then Amanda (8) needed some food thrown on her, and etc.

The food fight was in full swing when Brayden (7) entered the dining room. Kevin quickly initiated him into the fight with a huge bowl of mashed potatoes. Brayden just stood there and looked stunned for a moment. He acted like he was mad at us so we just kept at our fight.

Suddenly, he got a light in his eyes and said, "Hey, Dad." As Dad turned to him, he came barreling in towards Kevin with his stomach all puffed out and yells, "How 'bout another pack-o-nutty buddies."

And then he belly bucked his father!

We laughed so hard at Brayden and he laughed too. In fact, he laughed so hard that he had tears running down his face. (He got the idea off the Aladdin and the King of Thieves video. In the video the genie and Aladdin are fighting off the thieves. There is a big fat thief who uses his weight to his advantage against his enemy. The genie turns himself into a huge, fat farmer in bib overalls and straw sticking out of his mouth and yells that line at the fat thief just before belly bucking him to his defeat.)

There's plenty of use for superheroes!

Derek (21 months) has several uses for the word Spiderman. It refers to Spiderman the comic character. It also refers to any bug with many legs. Today he pulled my glasses from my face, poked my eyelids and said, "eyes, eyes".

Then he gently pulled on my mascara laden lashes and said, "piderman, piderman."

You never know what you can learn just from watching cartoons!

We were eating popcorn and Derek (9) was doing so a little too aggressively. Therefore, a couple of his siblings started teasing him about being a pig, hippo, etc. Malena (4) decided she knew better than the other kids which animal would best match our beanpole boy, Derek. Her choice? "A lamb with um, um, the um cut off hair!"

(If you have seen, Disney's "The Incredibles", there is a mini-feature on there with a shorn lamb. He is very, very scrawny with large eyes. All in all, her description of him fit much better than the more stout animals mentioned by the other kids.)

Being bilingual may come in handy if you are in Africa.

I was teaching Malena (5) about Japan and showing it to her on the globe. Kevin jumped in at this point wanting to point out the country in which he served a mission. He showed her the country and then tried to get her to remember the name of it. He asked her what language he could speak. He prompted in a slow drawn out way "Ko" and then "Ko-ree".

> This was when Malena was sure she knew the answer, so she happily responded in a low voice in the same drawn out way as Kevin had, "Go-rilla!" (Apparently she has watched Disney's Tarzan one too many times!)
>
> So, Kevin speaks gorilla if that ever would come in handy to any of you. Also, Kevin said that with the way letters are in Korean, the sounds K & G are the same and so are R & L, so if you look at it from a Korean viewpoint, Korea and gorilla really are the same word. :)

Then there were several instances where the kids show how to get a point across in whatever way possible or simply to share feelings.

It's okay to be upset sometimes.

> Daddy is away for eight weeks for his job. Two-year-old Patrik told me today, "Makes my mad. I want my Daddy!"

Some things happen again and again!

> Daddy is home again, but one day when Daddy left for work, Patrik (2 ½) put on a big pouty face and said, "I lost my Daddy again."

We can experience more than one emotion at a time.

Today Patrik (2 ½) told me this, "Mommy, this is my sad eye." Oh? "This one is my happy eye."

Don't be afraid to ask for help.

Sean (1) was discouraged because he had lost something he was playing with. He motioned for me to come with him. He led me to the pantry shelves and pointed. I looked and saw nothing. He seemed insistent that something was there, so I looked again.

"Sorry, Sean, I don't see anything," I told him. So he lay his body flat down on the linoleum floor and looked. Then he got up, pointed at me, and then pointed at the floor. So, I followed suit as told.

I never did find what it was, however.

Share joy and frustrations.

Sean is 16 months old and very bright. He won't say much, but he sure can communicate. (He says "hi" a lot) He uses hand gestures and different tones and pitches to his voice to get his point across.

Sean goes to sleep most every night snuggling with Daddy on the couch while watching sports with Dad. When the sports come on and throughout the whole time, he cheers, claps hands and squeals with delight. If the screen shows only stats and scores and no action, he screams impatiently until the action returns. He is turning out to be my biggest sports nut yet!

Make sure you are always being modest.

I had just gotten out of the shower and the phone was ringing. I grabbed a towel, wrapped it around myself and answered the phone. It was a quick call, but Sean (1 ½) came before I was done on the phone and started jabbering at me. I hung up the phone and asked him what the problem was. He beckoned me to follow him into the bedroom where he grabbed a handful of clothes from the laundry basket. He intoned in many sounds that I needed to put them on!

Kids are a genuinely persistent lot. You should not let anyone tell you that you can't do something you know you can do.

Brayden (3) found a plastic knife at Mormor's house and said he was going to "cut a fly". I told him "you can't cut flies because they fly away too fast."

Brayden spotted one on the counter and started to drag a chair over to it. I told him not to bother because the fly would be gone before he got to it anyway. Needless to say, the fly was still there as Brayden climbed up on the chair.

I began to say, "You just can't cut a fly." All I said was "You just" and had to stop mid-sentence because I turned in time to see Brayden cutting that fly.

Please goes a long way.

Sean (3 ½) had had plenty of food to eat and yet he still insisted on saying, "Mom! I'm hungry!" every five minutes.

When he once again started with, "Mom!..."

I interrupted by saying, "Don't say it! Don't say it!"

Sean then says, "Mom? May I please say it?"

Never say you don't like something.

Malena (1) doesn't care for peaches. I tried to give her a bit of one as I was cutting some up to eat along with dinner. She refused it as many times as I offered it. Then as I dished up her plate, I put one slice on there to see what would happen. When she discovered it, she placed it on the side of her plate. Then on second thought, she shoved it farther away. She munched along happily on chicken and noodles until she looked at it again, at which time she had to push it even farther away from herself.

She remained content until we passed the bowl of peaches to Brayden (11) who sat next to her. At this point, she took her fork and tried to shove the bowl away from her.

The funny thing is, a couple hours later, Kevin had her eating his peaches. So, the moral of the story is...you can never really say your baby doesn't like something!

If you are determined, you can do whatever you think you can.

Patrik (17) is very excited to finally have gotten contacts. It was particularly rewarding to watch his first attempts at putting them in. He was fiercely determined to do so. He planned to succeed regardless of the cost. He pretty much tried ramming his contact clad finger into the center of his eye that he held open forcibly with fingers of the other hand.

The lady that was helping him out said (after he had succeeded) that when she first saw him she didn't think he was going to have success on this trip and that we would have to schedule another. The shape of his eye and the fact that he is a teenage boy led her to this conclusion. He proved her wrong, thankfully!

Technology can be pretty terrific. It is amazing how quickly kids pick up on all the latest technologies. They absorb it faster than the adults do!

Some things are easy to fix...

> Aunt T had been talking about how Uncle B would always get headaches when he tried to give up Pepsi. Later on, Patrik (7) wanted to know why this was so. I explained it to him and he came up with this solution; "Maybe he should get a brain transplant."

Everyone has to have surgery sometime, don't they?

> Yesterday the kids were playing with their plastic dinosaurs. I heard Sean (4) say that one of the dinosaurs had to go in for surgery for his stomach.

Everything's going digital.

> Malena took a picture with her toy camera, brought it to me so I could view the "display screen". Then she handed me the camera and says, "You have to download it on to the computer now." How's that for a modern 2 year old?

Even food is high-tech these days.

> On our long drive home yesterday, I handed Derek (9) and Malena (4) each a handful of a green vegetable to munch on. Malena decided

it was yummy enough to ask for a second helping. We couldn't help bursting with laughter when she very nicely asked, "Can I please have some more iPods?"

Later, I related this story to Amanda (15). I asked her, "So, what vegetable was she eating?"

Amanda must have been having a "blonde" moment because she responded, "I don't know…avocados?"

This is a generation of texters!

We were reading the scriptures last night as a family in Acts chapter 10. We often give each other a heads up when there is a JST or footnote of interest. When we got to the end of verse 36, Amanda (16) was pleased to announce, "Oh, this verse has a smiley!" Patrik (17) and Brayden (15) were quick to figure out what she was talking about…the verse ended with a colon and parenthesis :)

At times I get caught up in making sure things are just right, perfect, or by-the-book. My children show me ways to live with the fact that life is full of imperfections. If it weren't so, how would we grow?

The perfect Christmas tree…

We put up the Christmas tree with the kids' help. For the first time, we had a big enough tree to put all of our ornaments on. So, we divided up all the ornaments between the kids. The lower third of the tree was very heavily decorated. Brayden (2 1/2) enjoyed putting 5 or 6 ornaments per branch, so Mom and Dad did a bit of rearranging after the kids were in bed. (Side note: Now in 2008 I would say I would just as soon not rearrange things, but just enjoy the funny way the kids did it!)

Be daring. Maybe the kids won't always make a big mess!

Patrik (7 ½), Amanda (6 ½), and Brayden (5 ½) made brownies today. Patrik read the recipe and oversaw the operation. They got out the mixing bowl, egg beaters, measuring cups, all the ingredients, etc, and did everything themselves. I poured the batter into the pan for them though. Then they cleaned up the large mess they made!! It actually was not too bad considering the ages of the chefs! The brownies turned out pretty well, and they enjoyed it so much!

I learned that it is okay to let someone else do some things for you.

Amanda (7) is excited to potty-train Derek (2). She has taken him to the bathroom by herself a few times and knows just what to do. She loves to be a little mommy.

In fact, one day when I decided to quit, I asked who wanted to be the mom. She volunteered and no one else did. I asked her what she was going to do. She decided to make lunch. I became the daughter and helped. She made a fine lunch of tortillas filled with beans and cheese and a tasty fruit drink which she invented.

She tried to be strict with her brothers, but Patrik (8) had no intentions of being subject to his little sister and there was much murmuring. Sean (4) seemed to like the set up okay.

I thought it went quite well, especially when Derek started getting grumpy. I said "Mom" had to deal with him because he wanted her. She was trying to fold the laundry, deal with a disobedient child, a grumpy baby and watch a TV show at the same time.

Amanda wanted to keep being the Mom for a long time, but I realized I couldn't handle being a kid. It was driving me nuts to not be "getting things done." It was a good learning experience. Maybe I will do it again sometime.

Chapter 18: The End...Or Is It?

Well, that's it. It's over. I guess it really ain't over 'til it's over. Truth be told, I have many more years of this ahead of me. Sure, I have one who recently left the nest, but I also have one that is fairly newly hatched. I should have another 18 years worth of stories in...oh, about 18 years!

I have had so much fun with this, that I will surely make another book when I have gathered enough material.

What's that, you say? You can't possibly wait another 18 years for book two? Well, if I am truly to fill another book before then, I'll need more ammunition! Send your stories my way. However, I won't be making any grand promises. I may or may not edit your story. I may or may not choose your story to be included in an upcoming book.

Send your charming, funny, profound, interesting, awesome, hilarious kid tales to publish@completelee.com. Include your name, general area of the world, your story and your desire to be added to our contact list, which will let you know when future books come out.

ABOUT THE AUTHOR

Marika Lee Connole was born in Berlin, Germany to a Swedish mother and American father. She is the wife of Kevin Lee Connole and they are the parents of seven.

This fun book is Marika's second published book. Her first book is a book about childbirth, written with the intent to help those who have not had wonderful experiences with birth. Marika has also written many homeschooling and other helpful articles. You can keep reading more at her blog www.completeleeblog.blogspot.com.

Marika loves learning about nutrition and natural healing. She also enjoys playing the piano, singing and composing music. Her compositions include everything from children's songs to ballads, to silly songs to upbeat medleys and hymn arrangements. Cooking is a task that she enjoys, but certainly doesn't mind a break from it to sample wares from another's cook pot. Managing a large family has helped Marika strengthen her organizational skills and enhanced her use of creative budgeting.

You can visit Kevin and Marika's website at www.completelee.com, to view all their latest products and accomplishments. Included on the website are many free items, such as, recipes, sheet music, coupons, games, articles and golf information.

OTHER PRODUCTS

If you liked this book, you may want to check out these other products at www.completelee.com:

Storyoni

We have a hard time getting the family to quit playing this game! Sometimes we all get laughing so hard that tears are shed. Storyoni is hilarious, great fun! This is a game you can play with people of all ages. Anyone with an imagination and the ability to speak and/or write can play! (Suggested age range is from 2 to 100+)

Reluctant writers and teenagers love this game too. Use this game for homeschool, at home, as a party game, as a getting-to-know-you type of game, or at school.

Childbirth: Preparing for the Miracle

Nowhere is God's love more evident than in a newborn babe. Birth, the taking part in a new life coming to earth, is a wondrous and beautiful event. This book gives a very simple outlook on how your body works during labor and delivery. It includes practical advice that really works on what to do mentally to prepare before and during labor, and how to make the overall birth experience a spiritual one.

Music!

Need a new song? Marika has written 100's of songs for piano, children's voices, choirs, solos, barbershop, educational songs, silly songs, inspirational songs, hymn arrangements and more. You can find free and inexpensive sheet music and audios through our website.

Misc!

You can also find Family Home Evening (FHE) ideas, sporting events, puzzles, how to items, books, stories, and much more at www.completelee.com. Go take a look.